The Princess of Wales

The Prince and Princess of Wales on their wedding day at Buckingham Palace

The Princess of Wales

An illustrated biography by

SUSAN MAXWELL

QUEEN ANNE PRESS
MACDONALD & CO (PUBLISHERS) LTD
LONDON & SYDNEY

The pregnant Princess meets the Chancellor at 11 Downing Street

Created and produced by Robert Dudley and John Stidolph
Designed by John Robinson, jacket design by Bill Chouffot
© 1982 Antler Books Ltd
First published 1982 by Queen Anne Press, a division of
Macdonald & Company (Publishers) Ltd
Maxwell House, Worship Street, London EC2A 2EN
ISBN 0 356 07871 X

Typesetting and printing by Purnell & Son (Book Production) Ltd
Colour separations by Nickeloid Litho, London
Production control by Tonbridge Printers Ltd (BPCC)

Off to the Palace. Lady Diana leaves her flat for the last time

Contents

5

The couple at Clarence House on the night their engagement was announced

ONE

Princess Wonderful

"One can't really dance in a tiara"
THE QUEEN

ON a sunny day in July 1981, Lady Diana Spencer married Charles, Prince of Wales. The late arrival of this most cautious of Princes at the altar ended every single woman's impossible fantasy of becoming Queen of Britain and the Commonwealth but satisfied the impatience of Queen and country at the future King's progress towards respectable domesticity. Like politicians, Kings should be married. One might fancy a bachelor figure like mad, but would one trust him on the throne? Charles had chased and been chastened by many. To his frustration, the Protestants he desired were 'unsuitable'. Those suitable were Catholic. It was logical that if he were to follow the strict code of the royal game and find a well-bred girl of spotless reputation in the 1980s, he would eventually have to start looking in cradles.

A year after the wedding, seventeen Commonwealth countries would issue stamps bearing Diana's portrait and the Queen and Prince Charles would stand aside resignedly to allow the public and photographers a better view of the juvenile lead at any Royal Family appearance. In Brazil, where there are no laws to prevent commercial body-snatching, Diana's picture was being used on posters for razor blades and soap powder. A single, exclusive picture of Diana engaging in any pursuit from sneaking away from a dressmaker's fitting to pirouetting on her front lawn in gumboots, could be worth over £2000 when syndicated.

Why this engulfing craze, this 1980s-style cult following? The Royal Family has always eschewed the brash, gadfly elements of social change, studiously avoiding association with the American *glamorosi* and the European *glitterati* whose pictures are the common currency of glossy magazines. Rarely do they haunt the fashionable resorts or party with beautiful people. They do not need to; they are an exclusive set, entrance to which cannot be achieved by dollars or diamonds. Though, as Princess Elizabeth realised young, it was no guarantee of a good time. ''One can't really dance in a tiara,'' sighed the future Queen. But then, 30 years later, along came a Princess who seemed to think it perfectly natural to have one's tiara and boogie too. Her style is neither old, borrowed nor royal blue. At a Buckingham Palace garden party, she confides to a few guests (and they to a few dozen national newspapers) that she and Prince Charles have had a row—''when he comes over, why don't you ask him why?'' Then she goes on to tell another astonished cluster about the bruises on her *derrière* after a close encounter with her former kindergarten class. The royal box being the focus of every eye when she occupies it at the opera, she lunges at Charles, covering him with alabaster arms and kisses though waiting, admittedly, for the lights to be dimmed.

Disparity begins at home. She throws her tiara back in the vault and slips on her walker headset, sachaying around Balmoral's inner sanctum with her head full of Dire Straits. ''She can't hear us coming,'' says a bemused Queen Elizabeth. ''So she walks straight past us!'' Diana's informality and refusal to observe protocol for its own sake raises both eyebrows and grins from her in-laws. The Queen, whose self-restraint is legendary, has been seen to give a little hop, skip and jump while conversing on the hoof with Diana. Parallels exist. When the Duchess of York (now the Queen Mother) was unpardonably late for royal dinners, crusty King George V coughed forgivingly: ''You are not late my dear, we must have sat down two minutes early...'' Beauty and charm can get away with what, by Windsor standards, would be adjudged murder.

Handshakes come in bulk for the Windsors. Every time a member of the Royal Family steps out on business, he or she must be braced for the fervent clasp of thousands. The Queen copes with a gentle touch of the palm which delivers a 'don't squeeze' message. For added protection, few royal ladies embark on any handshakeathon without gloves. Diana is seldom seen with them.

Her dressmaker, her hat maker, all those responsible for her wardrobe, say she knows exactly what she wants and does not waste time with anyone else's taste (though she might pop on John Boyd's hats for other famous clients in one of her very human star-struck moments). She has her own sense of drama which instinctively and unfailingly selects the right outfit for the right occasion. She is Scarlett O'Hara for the theatre; a tartan lassie at Braemar; a candy-striped My Fair Lady with boater at Royal Ascot; Anna Karenina with Russian hat and muff when the

The Princess learning to cope with handshaking well-wishers during her tour of Wales

snow falls. Unlike other royal dressers, she takes calculated risks with her theatricality. And her fashion lead is slavishly followed by working-class teenagers, the *Mesdames* of Belgravia and, most astonishingly, her mother-in-law, who arrived in Australia wearing—of all things for a Queen—a saucy boater hat.

She also takes risks, given that anything she says in public will be reported, with her repartee. In Wales, where she was proclaimed as 'the flower in the Royal forest', she might ask an elated child if it could speak Welsh. The child rattles off a string of Gaelic praises to be told wryly, "all right, no need to show off..." Showing her engagement ring at yet another garden party, she giggles: "The other day I even scratched my nose with it. It's so big—the ring, that is." Buying herself a riding hat when she has at last been persuaded to remount after eleven years' absence from the saddle, she is told by equestrian outfitters that she has a large size head. "It may be big," she snorts in a self-effacing moment, "but there's not much in it."

There is not much, nevertheless, that slips past it. To say that she wears the pants in the Wales household is hardly fair, particularly since her husband so often wears the kilt. But, during the post-honeymoon press conference in Balmoral, few could miss the subtle change in dominance. In their television interview the night before the wedding, Charles had provided the banter, Diana barely said 'boo'. Less than a month later, he seemed unable to answer a question without first seeking the approval of her eyes. The 'shy' young woman who was considered by some to be too meek for a man who enjoys authority, arrived in his life without a whimper. More a doe-eyed air of devotion which carries its own style of command. When he goes away on business, it is Diana who drives him to the royal train. She keeps telephonic track of his every move thereafter.

She has a confident tongue, never lost for a witty reply or, when called for, a put-down. To photographers who presented her with a bouquet at Balmoral: "Bought on your expense accounts, I suppose?" To a designer whose nervous chatter had overstepped the mark: "Now, now, back to your basket." To certain royal ladies who mistook her disinterest in horses for fear, she explained that she had a tendency to put on weight, and that "riding exercises only the horse's legs". To her husband, during a blazing row over his insistence that she—pregnant, or in any condition—should be obliged to tramp behind him on his eternal shooting expeditions: "You know I didn't want to come in the first place!"

The immense power that Diana holds over the public with her growing superstardom is likely to be an awesome phenomenon even for the Royal Family. They have been respected and, in their remote way, loved before. But singly none has been turned into a virtuous sex symbol. To the public eye, Diana soon became divine. But those longer in the Palace cannot knock it. With Diana's rise to dominance has come the biggest resurgence in the public passion for royal figureheads since the war. She is a figurehead, with a figure and a head tailor-made for the standards of the 1980s—for the cult of youth, health, good looks and clean living—making her as much the currency of glamour in Europe and the United States as in Britain. ''Movie stars were sometimes said to have a royal bearing,'' said America's *Time Magazine* when it devoted an eight-page spread and cover to Diana at the time of the engagement. ''Lady Diana Spencer brings star quality back to Buckingham Palace.''

This is an athletic, dancing, non-smoking, health-food generation. Diana takes long walks, tap dances, insists on having her bread brown and despises cigarettes. She wears her jeans as tight, her velvet jodhpurs as baggy as is fashionable.

The Queen has never been seen to kiss anyone but relations and even then, seldom in public. But Diana's is a kissing generation. She started her royal career in the manner she intended to continue, with a kiss on the Palace balcony that was watched by half the world. Leaving on her honeymoon, she gave a thank-you peck to the royal wedding organiser, Lord Chamberlain Lord McLean. In Egypt, she kissed Anwar Sadat goodbye, and in Wales she kissed Lord Snowdon hello. She makes a public practice of kissing the Queen, just as she kisses babies by the armload and her husband so often that he seems in a constantly puckered state. If the Queen is non-plussed by this flash 1980s style, she is aware that Diana's mail to the Palace is solid, sincere gush.

Her dressmaker suggests that Diana has charisma. A royal photographer puts her photogenic quality down to apparent vulnerability. Snowdon vows it owes nothing to retouching. ''She's so beautiful she doesn't need it.'' Her hat maker says Diana ''has such a bonny face no matter what she does—she could hang a wash cloth around it—she would still look nice''.

Diana enjoying Ladies' Day at Ascot

TWO

Limelight

"I'm a normal person"

LADY DIANA SPENCER

IN 1978 the ginger-haired flame of the Prince of Wales bluntly told the press that she was not the future Queen. "I doubt whether he has met her yet," she added. Sarah Spencer was one of the last people in the world with an excuse for such an ironically wrong statement. The Prince, striding into his 30s, showing more symptoms of the crusty bachelor than of the willing playboy, had vaguely known Diana Spencer, his former Sandringham neighbour, all her life.

He had politely steered her, she a blushing and pudgy mini-bopper, around the Christmas dance floor at one of those parties where the Queen dances with her staff. The Prince may not have been too aware of Diana, but he had met her more times than he had gallantly eaten curried snake for breakfast in the service of his country. She was totally aware of him, as were most unmarried girls in the English-speaking world. Earl Spencer joked at the time of her engagement that his daughter had been in love with Charles since she was a little girl. Then an old friend recalled—as old friends have a habit of doing shortly before they cease being old friends—"we were discussing the future and I asked Diana what she wanted to do. She replied: 'I would love to be a successful dancer—or Princess of Wales.' "

One might wonder if from the time Diana had her first adult 'meeting' with Charles in 1977, what may have looked like a teenage crush was in fact a sincere, patient campaign to win the man she wanted. People had always said she was the patient one; patient with children; patient with the press; patient most of all with the man who might one day reign over the Commonwealth,

13

but was in the meantime having trouble choosing a wife. When the Palace at last invited everyone to the wedding, the President of Zimbabwe composed a touching little verse, which could have been as fittingly addressed to Diana as it was to Charles.

> "It was worth waiting for the one most fitting
> It was worth sweating for the one most soothing
> It was worth living for the one most loving."

Diana, the happy couple told the world, came bounding up to Charles in a field at Althorp, the estate where the family had moved after Johnny Spencer inherited his Earldom. Charles was sister Sarah's guest for a shoot and it was the first weekend party to which Diana had been invited as an adult. The Prince and the little sister were both pretty giggly types, according to Sarah. They giggled harmoniously the whole time they were together. What "an amusing and jolly—and attractive—sixteen-year-old," thought Charles. Diana thought the man whom she must for the time being call "Sir" was "pretty amazing". She was mainly background music at the following dinner party, or she was meant to be. The Earl said he was aware of some kind of chemistry at work. "He was Sarah's guest. But it was obvious that Diana was the focus of his attentions." During the shoot Diana had stood, like some faithful King Charles spaniel, at the Prince's side all day.

It would be over two years, though, before Charles took her as seriously as she wanted to take him. In 1979 Diana spent part of the summer at Balmoral, helping her sister Jane (wife of the Queen's assistant private secretary Robert Fellowes) with their new baby. So it happened that Diana was with a royal picnic party when she saw her future in-laws in tears as the news of the assassination of Lord Mountbatten was broken. In the autumn of 1980 the invitation came formally from the Palace for Diana to be a guest of the Queen at Balmoral for the weekend. Less than a year later, she would stay there as the Queen's new daughter-in-law. But for now, she was plain Miss D Spencer on the flight passenger list and Miss Nobody to the group of newsmen who scanned the disembarking passengers at Aberdeen, expecting former girlfriend Davina Sheffield. Diana was picked up from the airport by a detective and driven to the castle without anybody noticing. Again, the photographers were lurking by the River Dee when she sat patiently watching Charles fishing for salmon the next morning. In those excitable days for Fleet Street, the first photograph of Charles with the lady who might be The Lady was the gleam in every picture editor's eyes. Charles, though, could sniff out a camera within a hundred yards. He spotted the Charles

Diana in her Mini Metro, surprised in the glare of a photographer's flashlight

squad in its lair and all that was photographed was a furious Prince and an unknown lady who had turned her back. The hunt was on but the romance was galloping faster. Charles later admitted of the first Balmoral days: ''I began to realise what was going on in my mind, and her's in particular.''

Charles certainly knows how to be charming. The bouquets of flowers and the hour-long calls from Balmoral started their determined pursuit of Diana in London. So did the press, for Fleet Street was soon on· to her. There was, in those heady bride-hunting days, a breed of men who made Charles their *raison d'être*. Instinct told them that this cautious, non-socialite of good family was so unlike his usual escorts that she could not be just another Highland fling. Diana kept smiling and saying nothing as the British press, soon joined by an even harder-bitten core of European *paparazzi*, clamoured daily outside her flat like Boxers at the Peking Wall. She enjoyed it at first. But like one of Charles's former loves, who was threatened with dismissal unless she dispersed the newshounds blocking egress at her workplace, Diana's kindergarten employers were irritated by the men who disguised themselves as roadsweepers in the street outside or climbed in through lavatory windows. Diana's politeness was, to use her favourite expression, pretty amazing. Princess Anne has sometimes commanded reporters in language that not even the Sunday papers would print. Diana stepped briskly, smiled briskly and always called the most braying member of the hoard by his name, prefixed with a schoolgirlish (even rather royal) "mister".

She did not even snarl after she found herself lured into the sunlight that produced those embarrassing leggy silhouettes. But next time she encountered the slightly more sheepish camera club, she kept her tight little smile. "I understand all your problems and there are no hard feelings," she was reported as saying.

The Palace could offer no protection. To an extent, the Royal Family realised this kind of trial was essential to test the colours of any new candidate for their ranks. At the height of Diana's harassment, the Queen was heard to mutter, "Well, she's going to have to learn to get used to this kind of thing. At least it's useful in that respect." Right throughout the courtship, Charles kept a personal vow not to be photographed with Diana. He refused to romance her in a goldfish bowl. So she was glumly holed up in her flat while he got on with his glittering social whirl, laying false trails with others on his arm and being 'engaged' to the odd princess he had barely met. The weekends at family retreats, the snug dinners in his Palace apartment or at the homes of close friends were Charles and Diana's only dates. He never once came to her flat.

Earl Mountbatten had been right in his prediction of how Charles would find the right woman. "He will not be seen with her in public. Very privately, he will try to win her round like any other suitor."

Sister Sarah takes credit as a match-maker. But greater powers were at work. The Queen Mother, having a formidable string of arrows to her cupid's bow, was determined that this girl should not slip through Charles's fingers for want of a private courtship. She invited the beleaguered young lovers to the sanctuary of her Balmoral dower house 'bonnie Birkhall'. The small Jacobite house in Charles's beloved Lochnagar country has neither gate nor namesign to show what majesty resides periodically within. "You have to imagine a house halfway down the slope of a teacup," Charles says of the little-known hideaway. It had been the sanctuary for Princess Elizabeth and Lieutenant Mountbatten when their Surrey honeymoon became a sightseers' circus 32 years before. Princess Alexandra and Angus Ogilvy honeymooned there as did the Duke of Kent and Katharine Worsley.

With her Prince on their first joint visit to Tetbury

When the Queen Mother is in residence, Birkhall fills with music and conversation and becomes ''the nicest place in the whole world,'' according to the Queen.

It did the trick for Charles and Diana when they disappeared there, leaving the press combing London and the Cotswolds for a blue Aston Martin or Diana's red Mini Metro.

More prosaically, they were some time later mooching around the vegetable plot at the home of Charles's friends Lieutenant Colonel Andrew and Camilla Parker Bowles when the Prince reportedly proposed. Sort of. It was a strangely hypothetical suggestion. ''If I were to ask you ... do you think it would be possible?'' he began. She started giggling. ''I immediately felt the immense absurdity of the situation and I couldn't help it,'' she told her friends later.

From the way he asked, he cannot have been sure himself. So while there was no engagement there could be no protection for Diana, nor any let-up in the paper chase. Diana was giggling a lot less in public now. But the press did not acknowledge that it was their pressure, not the 'shy' myth they preferred to ladle out, that had sent her chin sinking so woefully. Nearly 40 years ago, Lauren Bacall invented what was celebrated as 'the look'. As a nervous nineteen-year-old, she found herself playing opposite a worldly man many years her senior, Humphrey Bogart. Bacall told me recently: ''I realised that one way to stop my head from trembling was to keep it down, chin low, almost to my chest, and to look up with my eyes. It worked. It turned out to be the beginning of 'the look'.'' Unlike Bacall, Diana, treading carefully into an infinitely delicate romance, was not attempting to get her face on to the front page. She was not born with the chin-down caution of a nervous cat. Legend has it that she once tipped the mast of the Prince of Wales's windsurfer at Cowes, ducking the British heir in the icy sea.

But midway through her nineteenth year, there she was with a chin that had descended pectorially so low that her boarding-school posture was an habitual stoop. 'Shy!' declared the headline writers, delighting in the rhymes they could make by abbreviating her name. 'Shy Di!' So Lady Diana's look and the accompanying explanation became a self-perpetuating myth repeated in the reams of newsprint that wrapped itself around the royalist world. If she was starting to look shy, there was a certain confusion between cause and effect. Said an old friend: ''She never used to put her head down. Diana was literally ducking the press.''

Neither did she have a firm, non-hypothetical proposal to

make all this exhausting marlarkey worthwhile. The story of clandestine canoodlings in the royal train, a complete fabrication on the part of a Sunday paper, was so far off the rails that the Queen demanded a retraction. No apology was made. Fiction and faction continued unabated. Diana's mother, Mrs Shand Kydd, sent a scorching missive to *The Times*. ''...May I ask the editors of Fleet Street whether, in the execution of their jobs, they consider it necessary or fair to harass my daughter daily, from dawn until well after dusk?...''

The Prince, according to those who knew him, was not coping that well himself. He had left Diana to tour India, and though it had been a gruelling tour, his nervier than usual mannerisms suggested torments unrelated to the human misery that brought tears to his eyes in Calcutta. Back in the jungle of London, where the relentless tom-tom of rumour pounded on, the Queen was testy at questions about the state of the nation's heir and matrimony. ''Even I don't know what's going on,'' she said. Presumably, neither did Diana. She could only speak to her action-prince if he got lucky with the Indian telephone system.

Leaving his hosts and the press behind, Charles tramped into the Himalayan foothills. He walked for days, lonely as a cloud, with two detectives trailing behind. He seemed to be thinking things over, and by the time he returned to his family for the Christmas that saw Sandringham media-besieged, he had almost made up his mind. He told his mother he would probably ask Diana Spencer to marry him.

Jolly good, said the Queen, or words to that effect. I'll ask her over for New Year and let you get on with it. But don't take for ever. ''The idea of this romance going on for another year is intolerable for everybody concerned.'' Another month was bad enough for Diana. At the suggestion of her mother, she planned to remove herself altogether. In Australia surely no one would bother her. This departure may have been a calculated ploy to get a decision out of her man. At any rate, she received a princely summons before her trip. Over dinner he proposed. This time he didn't say 'if', and she did not giggle. Gallantly, the Prince followed up the proposal with a telephone call to Diana's real father. ''Can I marry your daughter, Sir,'' he asked Earl Spencer. ''I have asked her and, very surprisingly, she has said yes.'' ''Well done,'' chortled the Earl. Only afterwards did he wonder what might have happened if he had said no. Diana had already made her instructions clear to papa, though. ''She has no qualms about the responsibility the position carries,'' mused the Earl later. ''She has never had any qualms about anything. She has known all her life what's expected of her ... she told me: 'I can give my love to the Royal Family. I can give my love to everybody. I have so much love to give.' When Diana told me she wanted to marry Prince Charles, I told her she must marry the man she loves.'' Replied Diana, ''That's what I am doing.''

Charles still wanted Diana to think things over, for he did not suggest cancelling her Aussie escape. She needed some peace to forget the romance of it all and ponder instead the frustrations and the eternal sobriety of the job she was taking on.

Ticketed as Miss D Spencer, Diana flew first class to Australia. Her entry papers specified her purpose as 'a holiday'. She passed unrecognised through Heathrow and two Australian airports before coming to rest at step-father Peter Shand Kydd's 4000-hectare sheep and cattle station near Yass. The property, known locally as Bloomfield, fronts on to the Murrumbidgee River on its lazy crawl to meet the Murray. The Shand Kydds usually winter there, preferring the joys of scrub-cutting in the Antipodean high summer to the cold of Scotland. This time they wanted Diana with them. ''I think she was having a very trying and difficult time with the press attention,'' Frances Shand Kydd

The Earl, Raine and brother Charles outside the Palace
Opposite: Diana outside Coleherne Court

explained later, with her genteel style of understatement. ''... it's always helpful to know there's a holiday and a little bit of privacy at the other end of the tunnel. She and I were very keen to have her last holiday as a private person together.''

The Yass farm staff became Diana's first bodyguard. There was peace at first. Diana even helped in the paddocks, happily bounding off and on a tractor, attacking the Bathhurst burr—a perpetual thorn in the side of Australian graziers. But the burr-cutting idyll was short-lived, shattered by an Aussie reporter's telephone call. ''G'day. Is Lady Di there?''

Peter Shand Kydd, who can acquit himself passably in Strine, said he was just a humble farmer in from the paddock with two constipated cows on his hands. ''You've got the wrong continent, try the Caribbean.'' But Diana's kangaroo courtiers would not, as they say, have a bar of it. Swarms of journalists camped outside Bloomfield and the station manager guarded the gate with a shot-gun. Diana and her mother fled to Mollymook Beach and there, in a cottage loaned by Charles's friends Lord and Lady (Kanga) Tryon, mother and daughter assumed yet another name. ''It was like a real family holiday,'' said Mrs Shand Kydd. ''Of course, we talked about Diana's future life. I would be a very abnormal mother if we hadn't.''

21

Peter Shand Kydd described the twelve-day Australian 'holiday' as a nightmare. His secret manoeuvres—though not as successful as those of his fugitive step-brother Lord Lucan—were nevertheless effective enough to have even Charles given what Australians call the bum's rush. When someone called from London claiming to be the Prince, the Yass men still gave nothing away. "But I am the Prince of Wales," the voice persisted. "Oh yair? How do I know?"—"Now look here, I really am ..." The enraged Prince eventually got through by another line.

Good things come to princes who wait. Charles had waited longer for a wife than any other Prince of Wales, even if he had not taken monastic vows while he killed time. His list of acknowledged girlfriends had taken a third of a page in Anthony Holden's *Charles—Prince of Wales*. Diana Spencer was only sixteen at the time of compilation, so she was among the few aristocratic eligibles not on Holden's roll call. Nevertheless, Britons were fairly certain who their next Queen would be by the February evening when Diana was drinking champagne at a secret royal dinner party. Diana would become the 32nd member of the immediate Royal Family in July; her baby bringing the Windsor total up to 33 less than a year later. If Diana thought about it as she made her curtsey to the royal ladies that night, she might have marvelled at fate. As an Earl's daughter, 38 categories of British women had titles superior to her own. In six months, all but the two most senior women in the country must drop her a curtsey on public occasions. Until she became Charles's escort, nobody had even bothered with her 'Lady' label.

The ring, as every souvenir shop in the country would attest before spring, was a great knuckle of sapphire, surrounded by large diamonds. The London jewellers Garrards had supplied it at very short notice for a figure guessed to be about £30,000. With the kind of tight lips that long ago earned their royal warrant, they were rock firm in keeping the commission and the cost a secret.

An exclusive pre-engagement picture of the sweethearts might have earned tens of thousands of pounds. But the nearest anyone came was a picture of Charles's and Diana's cars, prettily nose-to-nose in one frame. Charles stole one of the marches of his life over the press when he and Diana walked into the watery sunshine together on February 24 at the Palace. They faced the cameras and flashed their diamonds back, smiling, one shudders to say, radiantly. A poignant figure in the crowds outside the Palace gates, Earl Spencer clicked away with his camera.

The Palace photo-call on 24 February 1981

Diana was now a professional royal fiancée, the closest thing possible to being royal. Nervous strangers might drop a curtsey. Or a clanger, calling her Your Highness, even Your Majesty. On one of her first outings as the royal fiancée, a schoolboy bowed and kissed her hand, even though she warned him he might never live it down. Worse things could happen to a chap. She had to start dressing in a royal fashion. After all, she was living in a palace and had her own detective.

Stranger things were happening. She was becoming a folk heroine. Royalty had made itself a remote, if revered, institution in Britain. Suddenly, here was an almost-princess who might be seen sucking a Coke can; who had worked for a living; who dinged her car. She was human. She rekindled a notion in unromantic times that Cinderella might indeed become a princess. Charles was Prince Valiant, jumping from planes and involved in much derring-do but he did not strike a chord with youngsters who did not ride with the Beaufort Hunt but liked their stereo loud. Diana did. Now Diana-fever was sweeping London. Girls in sailor suits, chain-store versions of the Bellville Sassoon creation, mobbed the pavements. Her hairdo was a neatly bobbed industry in itself.

23

Lady Diana and friends at the kindergarten

Kevin Shanley, Diana's hairdresser, was up to his ankles in the clipped locks of Diana imitators. The more hesitant could buy a Diana wig and the ring—or a more economical and thousand-fold tackier version was theirs for £8. The fiancée had only to be pictured in knee-length trousers to turn Britain into a sight resembling one great grouse shoot.

Personal appearances rivalled the Calgary stampede. Two nuns, present at one of Charles's polo matches, hitched up their habits and galloped to join the Di-gazing throngs who formed a semi-circle in front of the members' stand. The commentator begged vainly for the country to do its duty to the hacked-up turf. "Please find your divot and tread it, ladies and gentlemen, there is a polo match going on, you know ... now, really ..." At Diana's first garden party, a Di-sasterous hat did not stop palace guests from abandoning the Queen and stiff upper lips to stand on chairs for a look at the future Princess. There was a certain universality about her looks—something she has since shed with her puppy fat—that spawned Diana-imitation as a minor industry. Models in Europe and America painted and pouted themselves into reasonable clones, peered up through their lashes and sold chocolates. When Charles toured New Zealand and Australia soon after the engagement, the old kisses-for-Charlie routine by photographers

24

Prince Charles and supporters in the paddock at Sandown

was *passée*. The Prince confessed he was pining for Diana, so those noble chaps from Fleet Street stepped in and generously provided him with what they thought was the next best thing—Di-lookalikes in bulk. Five of them swarmed around Charles on a New Zealand walkabout; the picture was a great success all over the world, though the joke was wearing thin for Charles. He consoled himself with long telephone calls every night to the real thing.

He had glibly bantered in February about being in love, ''whatever in-love means''. But the farewell scene at Heathrow airport had been an emotional epic by royal standards. In a kind of reverse *Casablanca*, the hero strode achingly on to his plane while the heroine wept on the tarmac. As the tour stretched on, the telephone calls became longer (the alleged conversations would soon provide the Charles and Diana love story with yet another fictional sub-plot—the great bugging hoax) while Charles was chomping at the bit to get home and start masterminding his own wedding. Back in England, journalists had toiled night and day to come up with a past scandal that might glare through the bride's peerless halo like sunlight through a cotton dress. The best they could come up with was that she had once been thrown into a pool, alas, fully dressed.

She had kept smiling during mawkish speculation about her chastity, a state which apparently made her a freak at nineteen. She had endured the gynaecological tests which assured the Windsors that Charles would have an heir. She submitted to *anorexia regina*, a diplomatic shrinking disease by which she appeared on millions of postage stamps six inches shorter than Charles. The only description of herself which raised her hackles was 'sweet'. ''I'm a normal person,'' the Lady protested.

Sometimes the pressure was too much. Days before her wedding, she sat on the dais for Charles's polo match with a hundred professional lenses just yards from her face. Her nerves were already stretched tight by the preparations for her epic nuptials—Emanuels' seamstresses were coming unstitched about the amount of weight she was losing. At this polo match, she burst into tears and ran. The photographers ran after her. 'Shy Di,' nodded the press authoritatively. On that day, she was plain miserable.

In Clarence House and Buckingham Palace, she was doing a crash course in being royal. She learned the wave that would see her through a lifetime of waving: from the elbow, with wrist frozen like a Sylvia Anderson puppet. She learned the technique of smiling long and hard, with a grin that should never degenerate into a maniacal leer. In her in-laws, she had the most experienced tutors in the world. The art of wardrobe was also on the curriculum. She wrapped a curtain around her waist and practised walking with a train. She learned the rules for clothing: dresses must make her stand out; shoes must not make her tower over Charles; hats should not hide her face. She should look exclusive without allowing the critics to call her extravagant.

She learned to hold her tongue and her pen. Anything she said in public or wrote to indiscreet friends might be quoted. She lost the commoner's right to freedom of speech. As Princess Anne once said: ''You are always a bit on your guard. You know that because you are royal, anything you say might be given extra significance.'' But there were early signs that royal rules would not limit Diana's small-talk to the often dreary repartee of royal walkabouts. At her first garden party, there she was telling the curious throng about her visit that morning to her old kindergarten. The children had mobbed her and she had acquired ''more bruises on my bottom than you would think possible''.

THREE

The Spencers

"A lot of nice things happened to me when I was in nappies"

LADY DIANA SPENCER

EDWARD (Johnny), the eighth Earl Spencer, gave away Diana to Charles, the nation and the Commonwealth. More recently, he hit the headlines by taking away about £1 million-worth of art treasures from his collection—the finest in private ownership in Britain—and selling them. The reason was a sad fact of life: death duties. The irony in old money like that of the Spencers is that it costs a fortune to have it. There he was at the beginning of 1982, father of the Princess of Wales and owner of millions of pounds worth of Van Dycks, on his knees to the local council for a grant to do up the bathroom of a tenant's cottage. To establish a fund to service Althorp's £70,000 maintenance bill and to ensure that death duties should not cripple the Countess and the Spencer heir upon the eighth Earl's death, the odd Van Dyck, Kauffman and antique wine cooler has to be packed off overseas or to the museums who can afford them. Raine, Countess Spencer (the Princess of Wales's stepmother), is an old hand at tossing out the old to prepare for the new, and it has been said that the state of Althorp has always reflected the changing fortunes of the family and, moreover, of its marriages. They might have been lucky with Diana as a crowd-draw to the stately home, said the practical Raine at the time of the controversial art sales. "But the extra weight (of visitors) has cracked the library ceiling."

In 1975 Viscount Johnny Althorp became the eighth Earl Spencer. Althorp, the country seat, was his domain. He moved Diana, her two sisters and her brother to the huge Elizabethan mansion near Northampton. It must have seemed like moving into an art museum. They got used to the great Van Dycks, Woottons and Gainsboroughs lining the walls as casually as pop star pin-ups. They learned to accept visitors crunching daily across the gravel forecourt and into their stately pile.

Despite recent art sales by the Earl and his Countess, there is still plenty more where it came from, and today visitors pay £2 to gasp at the treasures. There are centuries-old porcelains, marble busts of the famous, who just happen to be Spencer ancestors. The entrance hall is a haze of horsey canvases, recalling the family's passion for field sports. The great picture gallery is festooned with Lely's beauties of the court of Charles II, reflecting a healthy Spencer interest in indoor sports. Visitors cannot buy Charles and Diana souvenirs, the Countess runs one of the few gift shops in the country which does not stock them. But Lord Spencer has opened Althorp's wine cellars for tourists who care to put money where their Margaux is.

Sixteen generations of Spencers have made Althorp one of Britain's most consistently occupied stately homes. The first Sir John Spencer bought the core of Althorp in 1508 and succeeding generations have altered it in the Elizabethan, Restoration and Georgian styles. It is bigger than most of the royal residences that Diana now stays in. Her family can live in an apartment at Althorp, undisturbed by the stream of visitors that has doubled since the country seat became a modern temple of Diana.

Royal Doulton adds Diana to their collection

At polo: a momentary distraction for the Princess-to-be

The wealth of Althorp is a legacy of a family which has farmed profitably, mixed politically and married powerfully for centuries. On one wall at Althorp is a modest Kneller oil sketch of a woman with a determined mouth. She is Sarah Jennings Churchill, Duchess of Marlborough. The Spencers' union with the Marlboroughs reinforced their arrival in social and economic terms in the 1700s. Already, the Spencer family tree had blossomed with royal connections and great names. But when Lord Spencer married Anne Churchill in 1700, the Spencers' march towards great prosperity accelerated. Anne's father, the Duke of Marlborough, was one of the most successful military leaders and social opportunists in European history. After he died, the widow Sarah engineered the transfer of huge estates to her grandchild John Spencer, also endowing Althorp with some of the Marlborough art treasures.

The family has often done well from judicious marriages. It has also prospered here and there from extra-marital unions. The beauty and wit of Spencer women did not confine itself to the twentieth century, in fact the diluted vein of royal blood in the family all flows from surreptitious unions in the seventeenth and eighteenth centuries. Three of Diana's beauteous ancestors were among those who fell in the bed of Charles II. The Spencer women's associations with the Princes of Wales has at times made them famous and infamous. Yet another Lady Diana Spencer made her mark by refusing a Prince of Wales. Her powerful grandmother, Sarah Churchill Marlborough, saw a gold-plated Marlborough future if Diana married Frederick Louis, Prince of Wales. She put up a tempting dowry and got the royal nod before Diana, who did not want 'Poor Fred', flounced off and married the Duke of Bedford. Spencer women seem as determined about what they do not want as what they do.

Two hundred years before the sisters Sarah and Diana were both courted by the same Prince of Wales, the precedent was set by two daughters of the first Earl Spencer. Henrietta and Georgiana Spencer were both involved with the hedonistic Prince George, the Regent. By the looks of the Kauffman portrait of the two sisters, angelica would not melt in their cupid mouths. But the frivolous sisters were the talk of British society. Georgiana made an economically brilliant marriage at the age of sixteen to the Duke of Devonshire. But by the age of eighteen she was an addicted gambler and could lose up to £3000 a night on the faro table. She was called the 'empress of fashion' and her extravagance was legendary. Her debts to Mr Coutts the banker

The marriage of Diana's mother and father at Westminster Abbey, 1 June 1954

nearly ended that financial empire at embryo stage. One man who shared her knack of falling into debt was George, the Prince of Wales, and so intimate was their friendship that during Georgiana's first pregnancy, people whispered that the child was his.

But the most enduring scandal in Devonshire House was the presence of Lady Elizabeth Foster. She was not just Georgiana's best friend, but also the Duke's mistress, and she bore him several children while the *ménage à trois* continued to shock Althorp and society in general. Georgiana was meantime accredited with having won the 1793 Westminster election for her lover Charles James Fox—she led a group of ladies who sold kisses for votes.

Sister Henrietta, Duchess of Bessborough, was chased passionately by the ageing Prince Regent 24 years after her sister's royal fling. But the 'grotesque figure' of the Regent was resistible to Henrietta. She wrote to a lover: ''Clasping me round, he kissed my neck before I was aware … he continued, sometimes struggling with me, sometimes sobbing and crying … that immense grotesque figure, flouncing about, half on the couch, half on the ground …'' She was nevertheless romantically active enough in her 51st year to boast in a note to herself: ''I am courted, follow'd, flatter'd and made love to *en toutes les formes*, by four men.''

Frances Shand Kydd riding with the Duke of Edinburgh on her daughter's wedding day

Not all the Spencers gambolled so recklessly. Many of the Earls were sage and serious art collectors. Diana's family tree may yet have a saint grafted on to it. A nineteenth-century Catholic black sheep, George, changed his name to Father Ignatius, and his followers in the Passionist Order are today proposing him for beatification, a step towards canonisation.

Diana's mother's side of the family does not sprout as many famous English names as the Spencer branches. But the Hon Frances Burke Roche (now Mrs Shand Kydd) has enough distinguished kin to make for offspring which genealogists classify as 'very interesting indeed'. Americans have hastened to call Diana 'the United Kingdom's one-eighth American future Queen'; within days of her engagement, they had confirmed her relationship to eight presidents, including George Washington, an eighth cousin seven times removed. The American ancestry came through Diana's great-great-grandfather, a clerk who became a millionaire stockbroker in New York. His daughter Frances married poor, but titled James Burke Roche, the third Baron Fermoy, despite her father's protest that "international marriage should be a hanging offence''. The marriage failed and papa decreed that if Frances's children were to inherit his fortune, they must not marry Britons. Happily for Prince Charles, Edmund Roche defiantly returned to Britain to claim the Fermoy title and fell in love with Ruth Gill, who happened to be a best friend and piano duet partner of one Elizabeth Bowes Lyon. Lady Elizabeth would become the match-making element in three generations of relationships between Fermoys, Spencers and Windsors. It was with Lord and Lady Fermoy that King George VI spent the last day of his life, shooting hares, and Lady Fermoy was rewarded for her enduring friendship with the post of Woman of the Bedchamber in the widowed Queen's household.

The Queen Mother's relationship with the Spencers also goes back to her Scottish childhood. Another of Elizabeth Bowes Lyon's close friends was Lady Lavinia Spencer. Lady Elizabeth's first match-making coup in this saga was the introduction of Lavinia's brother, Viscount Bertie Spencer, to a friend called Lady Cynthia Hamilton. Cynthia became Countess Spencer. When Elizabeth herself made a spectacular marriage to the Duke of York and found herself a reluctant Queen soon after, she invited her old friends into the royal household. Countess Spencer became a Woman of the Bedchamber. The King admired Earl Spencer and the two families were often together. As Master of the hunt, the seventh Earl rode over to the royal residence one day to be greeted by Princess Elizabeth in the doorway. ''Do please come in,'' said the little girl. ''But you'd better leave your horse outside.'' It was logical for the little Princess to play with little Viscount Johnny Althorp and for him, in time, to join the household as equerry to George VI. His post continued into the reign of Elizabeth II, and just before he left with the Queen and Duke on their first world tour, he proposed to Frances Roche, Lady Fermoy's eighteen-year-old daughter.

Thus the family that had the blood of George Washington, General Patton and Humphrey Bogart in its veins married into the blood of Charles II and the Duke of Marlborough. It was an auspicious start for Frances and Johnny Althorp's children. Lady Diana, the third daughter of the short-lived marriage, scarcely needed to marry into the Windsors to enrich her pedigree. Indeed, the Windsors were doing pretty well out of her lineage. Through the indiscretions of Diana's female forebears, Diana's children would bring back the blood of Charles II and James II, the Stuarts, to the royal line.

Even at their baptisms, Frances' and Johnny's children were

33

dipped in honour, with the sponsorship of royal godparents. Middle sister Jane strengthened the royal connection by marrying Robert Fellowes, a Sandringham neighbour who became assistant private secretary to the Queen. Diana has said that "a lot of nice things happened to me when I was in nappies". But silver nappy liners have clouds. Diana was six years old, Jane was ten and Charles barely out of his nappies in 1967, when the Spencer domestic situation changed overnight.

One hundred years ago, the suggestion that two daughters of a broken home would be seriously courted, and one married, by a Prince of Wales would have had aristocrats choking on their port. Divorce lost most of its stigma in society during the first half of this century, but the monarchy was longer hidebound with outdated standards than any other sector of society, even the Church itself. Wallis Simpson's divorced state was only one reason for her unsuitability as wife of the King. But in the case of Princess Margaret and Peter Townsend, his divorce was the only reason. Even though he had been granted a divorce as an innocent party, the romance with Margaret was doomed. The Queen, regardless of her personal feelings, felt obliged as head of a Church that frowned on divorce to continue a rearguard action even after the bishops had thrown in the cloth. Until fairly recent decades, the Honours Committee withheld or delayed decorations for divorced people. They were politely steered away from the presentation flow at royal mingles and 'guilty parties' could not be invited to Palace functions. George V had broken down some social red tape by admitting such moral lepers to the royal enclosure at Ascot for the first time. Even at the beginning of the reign of Elizabeth II, royal household staff whose marriages collapsed felt compelled to offer their resignations.

By dint of its players, the Spencer divorce drama was one of the more lavishly reported matrimonial cases of the 1960s. Frances and her husband were the sort of stiff-upper-lippers who never let their unhappiness show before the servants or the children. There were no scenes. Frances's overnight disappearance from Park House, Sandringham, took everyone by surprise. The new man in her life was Peter Shand Kydd. The Viscount and Viscountess had sheltered their children from their unhappiness, but there was no retreat for Diana, Jane, Sarah and Charles during the long and bitter fight for child custody. Newspapers delighted in the aristocratic procession that the Viscount had arranged to testify in his favour. Diana, according to a family friend, began the nail biting which remains to this day a lone vice. If the tug-of-love had

*The Spencer-Churchill connection: the Prince and Princess with
the Duke and Duchess of Marlborough at Blenheim*

any positive effect, it probably strengthened the bond of sympathy
between the Queen Mother and Lady Fermoy, Frances's mother.

The court judged in the Viscount's favour and the Viscountess,
soon Mrs Shand Kydd, retreated to Scotland.

At Althorp, the Spencer offspring were dismayed by their own
father's choice of a new partner. The Countess of Dartmouth was
nothing like Frances. She thrived on scenes, the more public the
better. To her credit, these were usually in pursuit of right, the
way she saw it. Marrying into the Spencer clan gave her the family
motto *God defend their right* to support her tireless drive to have
things done her way. Long before she became Countess Spencer,
her mink-trimmed flamboyance made her rival her mother's
prominence in the gossip columns. ''Publicity?'' she once
explained to a journalist. ''Of course I've chased it. I admit it
openly. But I am not interested in politics or publicity for its own
sake, but as a way of getting things done.'' Raine inherited the
whirlwind efficiency by which her octogenarian mother has kept
her status as one of the world's most prolific authors. The
daughter is intolerant of cumbersome tradition and sloppy
operators. She and her mother united in an effective campaign for
the rights of Britain's old people in the 1950s. Raine, then a
Westminster City Councillor, visited geriatric homes and joined
her mother in a pink fit. They forced the government to start an
inquiry into the housing conditions of the elderly.

Raine had virtually been born with a silver publicity handout in
her mouth. Her pa was rich, her ma was a recognised writer. She

was given an old Celtic name, for Barbara Cartland saw the Scots as the most romantic men God ever put breathless passion into. At seventeen, she was debutante of the year and she inspired more than one of her mother's virginal heroines. In true Cartland tradition, she married the first man she fell in love with. Gerald Legge was solid, rich and after the death of his father, Lord Dartmouth, she became the Countess. "He is the rock of Gibraltar and divine," she told friends of her husband. But when it was dead, it was dead. Tidy Raine had no use for old rocks. She is said to have moved her possessions to Althorp in a horse float.

Johnny Spencer, Gerald Dartmouth's old Etonian chum, was by now the Earl. Despite inheriting one of the richest titles in Britain, he was a sad figure, mouldering in his stately pile and contemplating the priceless paintings, porcelains and the death duties that threatened to spirit away the lot. His children were spending as much of their holidays as possible with their mother in Scotland.

But then along came Raine. Socially, the glittering Countess and her even more glittering mother were considered upstarts. The Spencer girls were not snobs, but the prospect of this Countess reigning over the genteel traditions of Althorp went down like a lead balloon. She, so trim and porcelain-skinned that people hissed the word 'facelift' behind her back, was in love with the lonely Earl and he was enslaved. In 1976 she moved in with him. Having named Frances as an adultress eight years before, the luckless Earl Spencer had a similar charge flung at him by the deserted Earl Dartmouth. But Raine got her divorce without the charge being proved, and the children sat tight during part two of their parents' romantic battles. When Raine and Johnny married, in 1976, there were only two witnesses. Even Barbara Cartland heard the news from Raine on the telephone. "Hello, we're married."

In Althorp, she had taken on a war. Rubenses were exquisite sticking plasters on cracking walls. The Long Library that housed some of the nation's finest books had a collapsing ceiling. The cruel economics of inheriting on the Althorp scale are illustrated when the Earl singles out a painting and tells his tour party of American ladies: "If I sold this now, I'd have to pay 60 per cent death duties and 30 per cent capital gains tax. Hardly worth it, is it?" Not least of the Earl's problems was his children's hostility towards their new step-mother. Raine told her own mother, "Whatever I do is wrong. I want us all to be one close family, but they are all so against me."

36

Diana's younger brother, Charles, Viscount Althorp, showing visitors round the family house

The children did their bit to keep the seat solvent. Young Viscount Charles might guide visitors around Lely's bosomly beauties and tourists used to walk past the future Queen of Britain sitting quietly on a corner chair in the state bedroom, just watching the shop.

In 1978, a week after the family celebrated Althorp's return to solvency, the 55-year-old Earl collapsed in the stable block. Doctors diagnosed a massive brain haemorrhage and told Raine he would not last the night.

''If you sit down and cry, you cry for yourself,'' she said later. ''The only thing I could do for him was to use my life and energy for his life.'' She had heard of a German 'miracle drug' so new to the market that it had not yet been tested in Britain. Through friends, she ferreted out the only compound of the drug in the country and persuaded the Earl's reluctant doctors to administer it. He seemed to recover (the drug, Aslocillin, was two years later approved for sale in Britain). Saving her husband had become a Raine campaign with double the vengeance of her old people's crusades. Ignoring rebukes from hospital staff, she sat with her comatose husband and sweet-talked, nagged and hounded him back to consciousness. When she played him a tape of *Madame Butterfly*, ''he just opened his eyes and was back,'' she recalls.

Apart from his hesitant speech and occasional exhaustion, the

Earl's recovery seems full. Since Diana's wedding, he and the Countess have become prominent first-night theatre-goers in London, where they keep an apartment in the same block as the Countess's former husband. They sometimes winter on the Caribbean island of Mustique, in a villa rented from Princess Margaret. They greet visitors at Althorp, where the Earl serves in the wine shop.

The daughters were not impressed by their step-grandmother's lyrical outpourings in what they called 'silly' books, and Diana's relationship with Raine was still overcast. Despite the restorative powers of her Puccini records, the Countess had different feelings about Diana's Police and Dire Straits albums, and they were banned from the Althorp stereo system. When Diana returned home to the pressless oasis of Althorp during 1980, she apparently preferred a house in the grounds to the family apartment. It was a bad lookout for Althorp and the Earl when, at one stage, the daughters would see him only if he came to London alone. During the rumour-rich period of royal wedding invitation postings, Diana apparently insisted that Mrs Shand Kydd would be the only woman invited as her 'mother', and the only mother in the family pews. So Countess Spencer, stunning in her Paris gown but solo, was seated well back in the masses while Frances and Johnny got along politely in the limelight.

The Spencer family vaults at Althorp

FOUR

Growing Up

THERE was something special about midwife Joy Hearn. The Viscount and Viscountess could have engaged the best obstetrician available. But Frances Althorp, pregnant in 1961 with the child she hoped would be heir to the family title, arranged to have Joy Hearn flown back from Canada to where she had emigrated three years before. In the old stone house that the family rented from the Queen, the midwife had delivered the Viscountess of two earlier babies. One had been the son who died soon after his birth. The gravestone 'in loving memory of John Spencer' is a sad little monument to that hoped-for heir in Sandringham churchyard. Everyone hoped that the next son would live long enough to inherit.

The delivery on 1 July was described by Joy Hearn as completely without complications . . . except that the perfectly formed little aristocrat was a girl. For the moment, the Spencers were caught unprepared. They had not allowed for such a contingency by having a girl's name ready. The new arrival, however, was totally at ease with her own destiny right from the start. She took happily to breast feeding and with a pragmatism vital to surviving the disciplines of upper-crust childhood, she calmly accepted first the midwife then the nanny as surrogate mothers. She slept in a cot in Joy Hearn's room for the first month of her life. ''I don't remember her ever waking me up at night,'' said the nurse twenty years later. ''She was breast-fed from the start and I think that helped.''

Diana was dressed in white for her first journey to the church soon after. Her Sandringham baptism was a tear-free affair. Unlike

39

the other Spencer girls, who are godchildren of the Queen Mother and the Duke of Kent (the son rated one better: the Queen is his godmother), Diana ironically missed out on royal patronage. That she would have to find for herself later on. Jane, the middle daughter, had rather stolen the expected baby's thunder a few weeks before by tripping down the aisle of York Minster as flower girl to her godfather the Duke of Kent and Katharine Worsley.

Park House is a huge Victorian dwelling which backs on to Sandringham cricket pitch, the 'Sandringham blue' door marking it royal property. Frances's father, Lord Fermoy, was granted the lease through his friendship with George V and the house later became available to the newly wed Viscount and Viscountess Althorp. So Frances brought her daughters up in the same house, enjoying the same Norfolk countryside and learning in the same schoolroom with the same tutor that she herself had. Park House, which has stood empty since her father inherited Althorp and moved the family to Northamptonshire, is full of bitter-sweet memories for the Princess of Wales. During Diana's first New Year at Sandringham, she took a step back into her not-so-perfect childhood by unlocking the blue door and stepping alone into the chilly, decaying rooms. Here was the classroom where the private governess Gertrude Allen called the roll. A blue tick went beside the names of Sarah, Jane and later Diana, who shared their classroom with a few local children. Here Diana was spellbound by lessons about kings and queens, not battles, according to the teacher she called ''Ally''.

A generation before, the same lady had been ''Gert'' to the children of Lord and Lady Fermoy. Frances had then gone off to boarding school and grown into the long-legged belle of Norfolk. She was sixteen years old when she met Viscount Althorp, sending this, the most eligible bachelor in the district reeling. ''I greatly approve of my daughters marrying men they love,'' Frances said 28 years later. Like daughters, like mother. Frances had married her man despite advice that she was too young, that the age-gap was too great and that he was already promised to the Earl of Leicester's daughter. At the age of eighteen, she wore her mother's tiara in Westminster Abbey. Because the groom was equerry to the Queen and because the bride's mother was one of the Queen Mother's closest friends, most of the Royal Family was there. Viscount Johnny was a godson of George V and Queen Mary and his family was steeped in royal ancestry, so it was a real possibility that one of their children might make a royal match. Viscount Althorp's services to the Queen as equerry ended soon

Diana Spencer as a toddler at Park House, Sandringham

after his wedding. He moved to Gloucestershire and studied farming in preparation for inheriting Althorp's great acreages. After Lord Fermoy died, Frances and Johnny moved into Park House, where all their children were born. The third daughter was a softie, eager to please, but could turn crabby when people mistook her gentleness for malleability. She liked to make her own decisions and, according to her father, she knew what she wanted in life right from the start. The maternal instinct was there early, too. She was pushing a toy pram around the lawn almost as soon as she could toddle. Her teddy had become an inseparable. companion by the time she was at nursery school. The same bear accompanied her to two boarding schools, a Swiss finishing school, a London flat and is probably now enjoying the high life at Highgrove.

If her parents had been imbued by their parents with the kind of discipline that had made the Spencers and Fermoys trusted friends to three generations of royalty, the rod seemed to have been spared on Diana. She was pretty, well-intentioned and charming enough occasionally to get away with murder, a recent example of which was a bucket of water sloshed over her husband from an upper deck of *Britannia* during the honeymoon. Just as George V had found Elizabeth Bowes-Lyon so charming that he ignored the unpardonable sin of his daughter-in-law's frequent lateness to table, the youngest Spencer girl was too likeable for anyone to

Diana, aged six, with her brother Charles

regard her misdemeanours as serious. Her father bought her a swimming pool and later a car and her own London flat. She had her own annual income and, at an age when more academically qualified children were standing in dole queues, she could afford to shop in Harrods.

Dianecdotes are rare. But as she grew up in an era of easily operated cameras, most milestones in her life have been preserved in celluloid. These pictures are now potentially very valuable. When Mrs Shand Kydd's house was broken into shortly before the royal wedding, Diana's mother's chief concern was for the safety of her family picture albums. They were, however, miraculously unplundered. She admits to being possessive about Diana's childhood. When she is asked to reminisce in front of a notebook these days she says: "Her childhood was a normal sequence of events. It just alters with the area you live in . . . or your background . . . I don't think people change, except because of growing up. I think the qualities that show almost before they walk are usually in their characters for life."

At her first school she was Diana, a popular girl whose academic progress tended to plod rather than canter. At Riddlesworth Hall, a preparatory school near Diss, headmistress Elizabeth Ridsdale remembered the youngest Spencer girl as "an entirely average pupil . . . the thing I remember most about her is

On the west coast of Scotland with her pony, Soufflé

that she was a perfectly ordinary, nice little girl.'' Being ''entirely average'' was not her only distinction—''she was always kind and cheerful.'' Faint praise. But it may have pointed to a dogged determination just the same. Being cheerful probably required some effort for a six-year-old perplexed by the sudden, inexplicable disappearance of her mother from her life. Everything had changed overnight in the big, breezy Park House: her father was distraught, a pathetic figure who went off with the shopping basket to buy groceries on his own (to the sympathetic nods of villagers who understood); Lady Fermoy had moved in to look after the children before the nasty business of divorce and child custody hit the papers.

Diana had been speedily removed to acclimatise to boarding school communal bathrooms, regulation dress and queues for meals. *Facing forward* was Riddlesworth's motto. By Diana's third year of facing thus, she had advanced in general regard as the ''girl who tried hardest, marvellously sweet and patient with the smaller children''. She also excelled at games and was, for the time being, fond of riding. (This fondness would vanish after a bad fall at the age of ten. After breaking her arm and her confidence, she would not sit on a horse until cajoled into doing so eleven years later by the Royal Family.)

Though their father got legal custody of the four children, they

43

saw plenty of their mother and their new stepfather. In school holidays, they commuted between Sandringham and the Shand Kydds' huge new farm in Seil, Scotland.

Father also did his best to restore a jolly household. For one of Diana's birthdays, he arranged a gay rout and hired a camel to take her on an exotic tour of Sandringham lanes. The boys next door, whenever they were in residence at Sandringham, leaped over the wall. It is hard to go one up on the neighbours when their name happens to be Windsor—but Park House had a heated swimming pool, Sandringham did not—undying friendship can be built around less. Diana, longer-limbed and more athletic by the year, was a frequent swimming mate to Prince Andrew and Prince Edward. She was a school champion diver, very proud of her ability to soar through the air with the straightest of legs.

During Diana's schooldays though, she and Prince Andrew, only two years her senior, were as thick as thieves. They exchanged letters while he was at Gordonstoun and she was at West Heath in Kent. According to her old Headmistress at Riddlesworth Hall, Diana was determined to follow her prep-school friends to the exclusive £3000 a year West Heath boarding school. Having made up her mind, the girl who ''always tried'' passed the entrance examination with ease. The old stone school was no spartan Gordonstoun. But it was not the Ritz either. The rising bell rings at 7.30 am, lessons continue until 7.00 pm, with an extra session on Saturday morning. West Heath prides itself on preparing girls for 'practical' careers and being Queen is apparently among such practical vocations. Princess May of Teck (later Queen Mary) made her own bed and slept in West Heath's utilitarian dorms.

Understandably identifying with prominent figures from the past, she was interested in English history. Like Prince Charles—though to a lesser extent—Diana probably discovered a certain fascination in finding out about ancestors. This interest must have been intensified in 1975, when her grandfather died and Johnny Spencer became the eighth Earl Spencer.

Grandfather, who died at the age of 82, had been as much an institution in Northampton as the ancient house itself. Bertie Spencer was an old pal of King George VI and Queen Elizabeth; his wife, Countess Cynthia, held the archaic title of Woman of the Bedchamber when her friend Elizabeth Bowes Lyon became Queen. As a child in knee socks, Diana had attended her grandparents' 50th wedding anniversary a few years before her grandfather's death. The seventh Earl had earned limited prestige in his lifetime for his prowess at the hunt. He had also stirred up something of a stately shenanigan in 1948, when he cleaned out several generations of Spencer remains from the family vault and cremated the lot, in order to provide ''bags of room for the rest of us''. The caskets in the thirteenth-century church at Great Brington had contained remains of two former Prime Ministers, and several former Earls.

The eighth Earl and his children nevertheless settled into their rightful home and Diana persevered diligently for two more years at West Heath. Lack of academic prowess apparently did not discourage a brilliant career in her imagination. Later she would cut out an encouraging newspaper article about school-room failures made good. She left school at the age of sixteen. The contents of her reports remain a closely guarded secret of the school and Diana's family. But according to Frances Shand Kydd, end-of-term reports on conventional academic subjects were likely to contain the words ''tried very hard''.

Her early gawkiness had given way to a grace that waltzed away with the school dancing prize; she was particularly good at tap routines. But Diana's greatest prize was the school service cup, an award for the girl who gave the most help to the school and her school-mates. She was even affectionately remembered by the kitchen staff, for whom she laid and cleared tables voluntarily.

Much has been made of the fact that Diana slept with a picture of Prince Charles, kitted out like a modern Lord Fauntleroy in his investiture robes, above her bed at West Heath. Headmistress Miss Ruth Rudge, a stickler for accuracy even though a wet blanket for romance, insists that the picture was there before Diana arrived and remained there after she left. Many girls who did not marry the Prince of Wales slept under it. A more relevant subject of speculation in the dormitory was Diana's correspondence with Prince Andrew. The second-in-line was growing into quite a dish and at the age of eighteen he was already riding the crest of Andrew-mania. Dubbed the Robert Redford of the Royal Family, he had quite stolen the limelight from Prince Charles during a Canadian royal tour.

Finishing school seemed a logical step after West Heath, at least to Frances Shand Kydd, who arranged a £1000 term at the exclusive Institut Alpin Videmanette in Switzerland. Up to 55 girls of well-heeled families regularly make the pilgrimage to Rougement at the beginning of the institute's courses. The school nestles in the picturesque Upper Sarine Valley, close to the jet-set ski resorts of Gstaad and Chateau d'Oex. Diana enrolled on a three-month course concentrating on French, domestic science, typing and correspondence. Like her international school-mates, she took the pledge to speak French as best she could at all times. Madame and Monsieur Yersin, the school directors, remember the sixteen-year-old as ''a pretty teenager, but not as outstandingly attractive as she is now. She was popular with both students and teachers. Her sense of humour was very lively.'' It was at Videmanette that Diana and her friends indulged in tooth-brushing contests, documented by photographs that came rather embarrassingly to light days before her wedding. Clearly, though, they did her teeth no harm. One of the fluoride generation, Diana has teeth that have barely been touched by a drill.

Her French also benefited from a brush-up in Switzerland. ''Lady Diana was a keen student in her French classes,'' the Yersins told me. ''With regard to her skiing, she was capable and enthusiastic. Her domestic science course entailed dressmaking and cooking. During the cooking classes, a wide range of Swiss and French specialities were taught—like cheese and meat fondues.'' In her dressmaking classes, the patron-saint of frilly blouses ran up a blouse of her own.

Switzerland obviously had its fun moments, judging by the photographs Diana's friends took of her convulsed with laughter and embracing classmates on the ski slopes. But it was a far yodel from the England she loved. Suffering what was described as a severe bout of homesickness, she finished with finishing school after only six weeks. But there may have been another reason for her premature departure. While she was polishing up her French and skiing at Rougement, her sister Sarah was on a ten-day skiing holiday with the Prince of Wales and the Duke and Duchess of Gloucester at Klosters. The *paparazzi* were as thick as snow and there was some unsubtle press speculation about the number of bedrooms in the villa shared by the Gloucesters, Prince Charles and Lady Sarah. News magazines with sensationalist stories flooded Rougement and inevitably made their way into the finishing-school common room. Diana may well have already started a crush on her sister's boyfriend and Prince Charles had seen the little sister recently enough to appreciate that she was no longer a child. But the Rougement rumour that Sarah was just a smokescreen and Diana was the Prince's real lady was totally unfounded. As usual, Diana said nothing. But she did not stay around long enough to provide more fuel for gossip.

Soon after Earl Spencer's remarriage, Sarah had shrunk down

Happy times at Videmanette

to size eight with *anorexia nervosa,* an emotional condition which causes young women to diet compulsively. She caught Charles's eye at Ascot and his continuing attention helped Sarah back to good health; she was apparently so much amused by the press attention that she kept a scrapbook of Charles and Sarah clippings. She enjoyed the prestige of being his escort and, inviting him to a shoot on her father's estate in 1977, Sarah revelled in her entrance on his arm before a dinner party in Althorp's magnificent dining-room.

But Sarah is a frank young woman and when reports declared a love match after the Klosters caper, she felt compelled, under duress, to state the nature of her intentions towards the British heir. The relationship was platonic, she stressed. ''I am not in love with him . . . and I wouldn't marry anyone I didn't love . . . If he asked me, I would turn him down.'' Reading the reports, her beau was embarrassed and hurt. But he must have admired Sarah's honesty and principles, just the same. She was one of the only girls whose name was not struck from his little blue book for breaking the royal ring of confidence. A guest of the Queen, she spent the following New Year at Sandringham and she remained

Charles's friend even after her marriage to Neil McCorquodale. In the romance of Charles and Diana, Sarah even claims to have played cupid. But whether or not Sarah's fall from eligibility after talking to the press distressed her, the lesson had been observed by Diana.

For the moment, though, it was career time. In another era, young women from a family as aristocratic and wealthy as the Spencers would have stayed home to pour daddy's brandy and embroider quietly for their hope chest. But living in Northamptonshire, witnessing the weekend flow of Althorp visitors and providing snippets about the first Baron's falconry or André le Nôtre's Versailles-style gardens, was not how any of the sisters planned to spend their limited bachelor days. And although the new Countess Spencer's industrious revolution had pulled the stately home out of the red, there was still no love lost by the children for their stepmother's racey style. They preferred to let her get on with it without them. The Earl, acknowledging that his daughters should have their freedom, laid the path for their comfortable existence in London. For Diana, he bought a £100,000 flat in a conservative block called Coleherne Court, on the Old Brompton Road. She was landlady and the rent paid by Virginia Pitman, Carolyn Pride (her old school chum from West Heath) and Ann Bolton provided a modest income.

The Earl's daughters had no aggressive drive for lucrative careers. Rather, they displayed a penchant for agreeable, uncontroversial jobs that would indulge their interests, prepare them for marriage and the respectable place in society each now holds. Sarah and Jane briefly held fashion assistant jobs for *Vogue* magazine.

Opposite: Diana's sister Sarah with her husband Neil McCorquodale

Right: A wary look from fiancé Charles's Aston Martin at Smith's Lawn

Below: At Cowdray Park polo. Diana sits with friends

Diana had claimed from an early age that children were her interest, her hobby and her ambition. Logically, she took them up for a living. First came odd jobs as a baby sitter and nanny. She listed herself with an agency and a New York couple, Patrick and Mary Robertson, interviewed her for the task of looking after their baby son while Mr Robertson was stationed professionally in London. ''She was so refined and so well educated that we knew she must be someone special,'' remembers Mary Robertson. Baby

49

Patrick adored her and Diana kept the job until the Robertsons returned to America. Her bosses were peeved one day, though, when Diana rang and said she could not come to work. ''I'm sorry,'' she later explained. ''I was being presented to the Queen . . .''

Three days of the week, she worked at the Young England Kindergarten. Kay Seth-Smith and Vicky Wilson had set up the fashionable child-minding establishment in a Pimlico church hall in 1970 and their clientele was delivered daily by a parade of sports cars, Bentleys and Rolls. The fees, for a thirteen-week term, are about £200. Diana said she got the 'assistant teacher' job through friends. ''I wanted to teach children and they said: why not come along? So I first started off doing afternoons and then I did whole days.'' She took the children through their dancing and painting routines, did her share of the mopping up and escorting toddlers on potty visits.

In the powerful tides of stylish London behaviour, she was keeping a confident, unswerving path of her own; knowing her own values and convinced they were right for her. How familiar, though in a less extreme sense, to the gentle daughter of another Earl in another era. This lady could charm every man that moved, but smilingly turned away suitors because she felt their values did not quite match what was good and right in her judgement. Elizabeth Bowes Lyon was very serious, even rigid, about emotional fidelity, for all her high spirits. She was not attracted by flirtations and it never occurred to her (said an old friend from her 1920s girlhood) that unmarried people should sleep together— ''holding hands in a boat, now that was courting.'' *

Lady Diana was a modern girl outwardly. But she retained certain old-world values and, like the Queen Mother, was able to cling confidently to them. Unconsciously perhaps, both women knew their own self-regard was more important than fitting anybody else's fashionable mould. In the end, their gentle self-assurance would make them as strong as the men they would support in times of crisis. The Princess of Wales might well be honoured that she has been compared by many people to the Queen Mother. But the greatest honour for Diana is that the Queen Mother has said she regards the comparison as a compliment to herself.

* From *Majesty* by Robert Lacey.

FIVE

The Wedding

"I vow to thee my country"

CECIL SPRING RICE

WHEN we are all in our anecdotage, we will point to the wedding of the Prince and Princess of Wales as a notch in the yardstick of world events that we can gloat at having experienced; like VE Day or the Moon landing. We will boast that we were among the one in every five people on earth who saw the bride leave Clarence House in an antique vehicle named—as if from some fairy story—the Glass Coach.

The noise, in the words of the groom who was woken early by it, was "indescribable". From dawn, when the great gipsy camp in the Mall yawned and rose to aching feet, the Palace had been under verbal siege.

Everyone, including She in her small corner of Clarence House, saw the groom clatter by, dripping with gold braid. Soon the girl who once wore knickerbockers and drove a Mini swept out in a coach packed with tulle and silk. It was the hour of a thousand cliches. The first glimpse of the most important 'bride of the century'; the last time she would be seen as the virginal icon Lady Di; the first sight of the dress for which dozens of Lullingstone silk worms gallantly gave their lives and for whose secrets the dressmakers had resisted a fortune in bribes. It was for Earl Spencer, clutching his little girl's hand and staring blankly at the blurred masses, the last time he had Diana to himself. Weeks before, he had stared into a glass of champagne and spoken to an Althorp tourist with the gloom of someone encountering an overcast crystal ball, ". . . I'm afraid I'll never see my daughter again, you know . . . they fix his schedule two years in advance . . . that's a big job she's taking on and I probably won't see her

51

again.'' From the wedding day, Diana's in-laws would be the family with first call on her time (in fact, the Earl did not see her for more than two months).

''More people here,'' he observed dryly, ''than at Wembley Stadium.'' ''When were you ever there?'' giggled the bride. ''Never,'' he had to admit.

Diana sat in her own haze. She was heavily veiled, as everyone had predicted she would not be. Royal brides, they said, threw back their veils. Diana had her own romantic vision and would not be dictated to by precedent. Traditionalists said the engagement ring, which had scarcely left her finger in six months, would be absent today. But if Diana could wear a £30,000 bauble with her dungarees at a polo match, it seemed ludicrous that she could not wear it with thousands of pounds' worth of couturier-shaped silk. It went beneath a cascade of orchids to the altar, there to be briefly removed while Prince Charles slipped the traditional circle of Welsh gold on her hand. Everybody had said that Lady Diana would promise 'to obey', just as Princess Anne, Princess Margaret, the Queen and even the most dictatorial Queen Victoria had promised their respective men. But even as Diana became the wife of the highest-ranking man in the Commonwealth, a determination not to be subordinate was clearly revealed. The Archbishop of Canterbury had approved. ''It's a

The bride of the year glides up the steps of the Cathedral
Opposite: The arrival of the bridesmaids

bad thing to start your marriage with a downright lie,'' he said.

As with everything else about the 'wedding of the century', Diana's advance up the long red carpet to the altar had been timed precisely. She had three and a half minutes up her flounced sleeve and neither Diana nor her father were smiling about the challenge of simply getting to the Prince on time. She gushed like a silken waterfall from her carriage at St Paul's and took off up the stairs as Lady Sarah Armstrong-Jones and colleagues fought to control the ivory river behind her. Waiting in the entrance of St Paul's, dressmakers David and Elizabeth Emanuel, found their client calm as they fussed over her dress and train. It was less than two hours since they and two seamstresses had helped her to dress at Clarence House. Miss Deborah Smythson-Wells, as they had code-named Diana, had been watching children waving flags on television and was in a happy mood. ''But when she saw herself in the mirror, she cried,'' said a seamstress. Emanuel and co puffed up the lace sleeves, checked the bodice that had been taken in regularly to keep pace with the bride's diet over the past weeks, and, superstitious to the last, they sewed the final stitch into the gown shortly before it wafted on its way. They packed Diana and

53

her father into the Glass Coach like two tulle-wrapped sardines and motored away to meet her at the steps.

Diana had been told that she was one bride who could not be late; too much depended on the precision of the timetable that day. She, however, decided for her own obscure reasons to observe that particular tradition, and legend has it that Clarence House staff were instructed to sneak around putting clocks forward on the wedding day. She would trot away happily in the Glass Coach believing she was a fashionable few minutes late—dead on time.

The moment the coach clattered on to the Mall, the long veil over the secret of The Dress was lifted. Details flashed around the world in time to make the front page of papers 13,000 miles away and twelve hours ahead (where women had pressed their poshest nighties and sat up until midnight with the sherry). It was a trademark of the neo-romanticism that the royal love affair had kindled all over the world. The huge crinoline skirt, puffed by one hundred yards of netting, billowed like something Charles was used to leaping from aeroplanes with. The 44 yards of silk had been dyed ivory to suit the bride's complexion and to prevent the dress from turning into a glaring blob under television lights. Diana's trademark bow—copies of which would soon adorn millions of blouses and dresses—rested below the ruffled neckline on the boned bodice. It was a compromise plunge, the result of some nail-biting by the wearer and the designers. The trio had never conceded that the black dress of Goldsmiths Hall fame was unsuitable. But they had no wish to repeat the controversy. In the eyes of millions, here was one of the world's few surviving chaste twenty-year-olds, being joined in marriage with the future titular head of their church. Only Diana and her immediate dressmakers knew the secret of what was inside the pink bags emblazoned with the Prince of Wales crest that were discreetly delivered to Clarence House on July 28.

But like everything else about the dress, the neckline showed a political adroitness that would have done credit to Diana's in-laws. The V managed to expose a nice amount of flesh but an old-fashioned froth of ruffles tempered the effect. Appropriately for a bride with more British blood than her new kinfolk, the dress was entirely made of British material. In deference to her own family's complex politics, she had cleverly 'borrowed' from each of her divorced parents. Her mother's diamond clusters dangled from her ears. A Spencer tiara anchored the veil. Diplomatically too, her satin slippers hardly added an inch to her height.

As if getting from the Cathedral steps to Prince Charles in the moments allowed with a 44-yard silk handicap were not challenge enough, she had the additional responsibility of a father who, in the obscure brand of understatement peculiar to his class, "enjoys indifferent health". Later, Earl Spencer admitted that it was Diana who had supported him up the aisle, not vice versa.

"Here," as the Archbishop told the congregation, "is the stuff of which fairy tales are made: the Prince and Princess on their wedding day. But fairy tales usually end at this point with the simple phrase 'They lived happily ever after'. This may be because fairy tales regard marriage as an anticlimax after the romance of courtship. This is not the Christian view. Our faith sees the wedding day not as the place of arrival but the place where the adventure really begins . . . Those who are married live happily ever after the wedding day if they persevere in the real adventure, which is the royal task of creating each other and creating a more loving world . . . All couples on their wedding day are 'royal couples' and stand for the truth that we help to shape this world and are not just its victims . . . This is our prayer for Charles and Diana. May the burdens we lay on them be matched by the love with which we support them in the years to come. And however long they live, may they always know that when they pledged themselves to each other before the altar of God, they were surrounded and supported not by mere spectators but by the sincere affection and active prayer of millions of friends . . ."

Millions of friends cried at that breathless bride who muffed her lines and almost married her father-in-law; at that sobbing royal great-grandmother in the feather hat to out-do all feather hats. How many realised, though, to what extent the Princess had already fulfilled the promises contained in the hymn she chose herself:

> I vow to thee my country—all earthly things above—
> Entire and whole and perfect, the service of my love,
> The love that asks no question: the love that stands the test,
> That lays upon the altar the dearest and the best:
> The love that never falters, the love that pays the price,
> The love that makes undaunted the final sacrifice.
> *Cecil Spring Rice*

Out on the Cathedral steps again, the groom's lips said "wave now". The Princess of Wales, for this time at least, obeyed. Up went the slender arm, fingers glinting with a gold band. Up went the cheers all along the triumphant route home.

A thousand clichés were of course yet to come, indeed they have not died yet. But that day, bells tintinnabulated, hats frisbeed skywards and crowds surged to claw at the Palace gates like ancients imagining this touch of divinity might cure their scrofula (a 62-year-old Hertfordshire women had actually regained her long-lost sight in time to watch the wedding). Few, other than those with telescopic lenses and the family on the balcony itself, saw the couple's lingering kiss in the wings but minutes later, everyone saw it on the balcony. Lip-readers swore red, white and blue that the debonaire swain asked permission, the unverifiable dialogue running along the lines of Prince Charles: ''Well, how about it?'' The Princess: ''Why ever not?''

The wedding breakfast was simple. The cakes, all sixteen of them, were lavish. The Emanuels were triumphant, already telling all at a press conference before the happy bride was off on honeymoon in a rather more subtle Bellville Sassoon suit. No, the

Mutual support

The bride and groom on their triumphal journey back to the Palace

Prince had not told the Emanuels that he loved the dress but ''you could tell by the way he looked at her''.

The Princess of Wales's going-away hat was a jaunty feathered tri-corn. Some said the John Boyd design was a salute to the Queen Mother. Probably, it was yet another tribute to the Prince of Wales's plumed crest, the summer craze which had, in the weeks before the wedding, left hundreds of African ostriches running around bare-tailed.

A consolation for the bereft Earl Spencer was that he was one father who would not have to foot the bill for a daughter's lavish nuptials. The British taxpayer forked out cheerfully enough for its part, but much of the cost, including the bride's gown and trousseau, was covered by cheques signed by the Queen herself.

When the Queen and Prince Philip arrived to honeymoon at Lord Mountbatten's country retreat at Romsey in 1947, part of the house was still annexed as a hospital and the war-wounded turned out to greet them. Charles and Diana arrived at Romsey station having not read the British Rail magazines thoughtfully provided in the same royal train in which they had not held secret

love trysts. Neither would they suffer the sightseers who had driven the royal honeymooners to the solitude of Scotland 32 years before.

The army of newshounds who surrounded the Hampshire retreat was exceeded for once by security people mooching up trees and down dales. They had dammed the little river Test to stop anything but water flowing past, which may explain why Prince Charles had no luck fishing there the next day. Air space above the 6000 wooded acres was out of bounds to the American newsmen who hired a helicopter and even the local milk vendor's float was cased before it could deliver the Prince's pinta. On their first tranquil day for months, the couple relaxed by the pool and drank champagne. They probably read about themselves in the newspapers. Charles rowed his wife up and down the Test on that lazy Thursday afternoon and a skeleton staff served them meals in the chandeliered splendour of a dining-room where four Van Dycks and a bleary-eyed Emma Hamilton gazed at them from the walls.

If Diana thought she could quietly hold her husband's hand and let the world pass by for long, she had married the wrong man. Palace pressure, or the intoxicating presence of his wife, had persuaded him to eschew polo for the length of the honeymoon at least. But the cockpit of an aeroplane bound for Gibraltar proved too great a temptation for Charles.

The Rock was stirred but not shaken by an ear-splitting display of pro-British patriotism during the short time it took the honeymooners to drive the one and a half miles—every inch screaming—from the airport to *Britannia*.

In practised royal style, the honeymooners managed to seem oblivious to the political spectre hanging over a love-barge anchored in disputed waters. They were determined to occupy themselves with the pleasure of being alone with about 300 crewmen, bandsmen and personal staff. An informal flotilla followed the parting yacht and as Rod Stewart's *We are Sailing* filled the straits, the Princess snuggled into the crook of her husband's arm and had a little sob.

The honeymoon was one of a lifetime of cruises on board the Royal Yacht for Prince Charles. But it was the first on which he would be sharing a berth. Amazingly, the most envied yacht in the world has only single beds, an oversight which had been remedied on the honeymoons of Princess Anne and Princess Margaret by lashing two beds together. But this honeymoon was one occasion when Charles, who has endured the same spartan

Charles and Diana leave for their honeymoon bedecked with Prince Andrew's balloons

conditions as most sailors, refused simply to make do. He and his wife had been showered with beds as wedding presents and a proper bed—not grandiosely canopied as at Broadlands but king-sized just the same—had been loaded on board *Britannia* before she sailed for Gibraltar.

For their honeymoon, he had promised Diana her first prolonged break from the public eye in over eight months. But to be simply floating in the middle of the Mediterranean was not enough to guarantee privacy, as Princess Margaret and Anthony Armstrong-Jones had discovered in 1960. Days after their wedding, the *Daily Express* had published a half-page picture of the honeymooners in the Caribbean. The caption, a classic in paradox, gushed: 'The sun, the sea and the young couple sitting side by side in the lee of *Britannia*'s funnel, with nobody at all to disturb them . . .' The *Guardian* had tartly commented the next day: '. . . except of course for the aircraft carrying the *Daily Express* photographer . . .'

The lesson had been learned. Press attention for Princess Margaret and her husband was just a drop in the ocean compared to the world's passion for glimpses into the private life of the future King and Queen. In preparation for the plague of airborn *paparazzi*, *Britannia*'s pool deck had been shrouded in tarpaulin and the cruise route was the best-kept naval secret since D-day.

A wave from Britannia *before sailing into the sunset*

Literally hundreds of photographers, journalists and television people were on honeymoon too.

As it turned out, the Mediterranean cruise was a masterpiece of the kind of stylish cat-and-mouse Prince Charles delights in. His staff had cased many Mediterranean nooks and crannies beforehand and stop-offs were chosen according to public ferry timetables: on more than one occasion, a lens-laden ferry would pull in just in time to see the yacht's stately stern vanishing into the blue. Charles, who is usually up at six and exercising fanatically, somehow managed to sleep late. While he napped in the afternoon, Diana, in her bikini, explored the ship. When she arrived, thus attired, on the bridge, the crew were barely able to concentrate. She was reportedly slightly less welcome when she found her way into the shower room. ''I'm afraid you should not be here, Ma'am,'' said an officer modestly clasping his towel.

On one of *Britannia*'s runabouts, the couple roared into several Algerian bays. Algerian boondocks were among the few places on earth where wedding propaganda had made little impression.

Another sun-drenched day passed on Crete, where Charles unloaded his windsurfer and taught his wife the rudiments of a skill she is unlikely to refine if she is to be in full sail with a succession of pregnancies. The yacht cruised via Rhodes and Santorini—of archaeological interest to Charles because the

61

sunken volcanic mass is reckoned to be the lost civilisation of Atlantis—toward Egypt.

If 270 seems a lot of chaps to take on honeymoon, the crew is chosen for qualities of invisibility. No one bellows, instructions are transmitted by sign language. When members of the Royal Family are on board, running is banned and walking is permitted only in rubber-soled shoes. Sailors are trained to keep their eyes straight ahead but lest they should subconsciously wander, the floor and portholes of the royal staterooms are raised above eye-level. Charles and Diana could eat like kings and queens if they fancied it. Culinary tradition on board decrees that the English chef presents every menu totally in French and a typical *Britannia* meal is this 1981 menu.

Suprème de Pintade Smitanne
Fèves au beurre
Chou-fleur Polannaise
Pommes Persilées
Mousse au Chocolat à la Menthe

The Princess, diet-conscious as ever, visited the galley to organise salads that suited the weather and the waistline. The couple took most of their meals informally on the verandah deck or in the sun lounge, where silent men in monkey jackets delivered the courses and vanished. Some evening meals were taken sitting together at one end of the 56-seater table in the royal dining-room. Their faces were reflected across the mahogany ocean, between napkins artistically folded into the lines of the Union Jack. In the ante-room outside, a string quartet played melodies to eat romantically by. Phosphorescence jewelled the ocean on starry Mediterranean nights.

There are things on the Queen's table that cannot be ignored, even when supping with one's beloved. Mid-table is a statue given by the Sultan of Oman. It is a humble camel with calf under a palm tree and, at about eighteen inches high, it is dwarfed by the fruit bowl. But every hump, every frond, every exquisitely detailed hair on the camels' backs is solid gold. The dates on the palm are chunky rubies. Then there is the dish the size of a wash basin from the State of Qatar; solid gold and so heavy that it takes two men to lift it. One of two great golden urns—presented by a grateful nation to Nelson's widow after Trafalgar—stands beside where the steward decants the claret. Naturally, there was no shortage of rare old reds and champagne. The Queen's marine cellar, deep in the bowels of *Britannia,* stocks vintages to make wine buffs drool. But Charles and Diana imbibed only delicately. Diana hardly

The Prince and Princess with the Sadats at Port Said

touches alcohol and Charles claims that he can get high on people and atmosphere alone.

After the solitude of the Mediterranean, Egypt was a hubble-bubble of noise, flags, bands, smells and coloured lights. Photographers sweated on the docks but only glimpsed Diana, who seemed to be thumbing a newly royal nose at pleas for happy-honeymoon shots. The Port Said party for President Sadat was the Princess's first opportunity to play royal chatelaine. She planned the menu for a dinner perfect in every detail, even if the late President's dicey tummy prevented him from eating more than a mouthful. Sadat was nevertheless entranced by the suntanned beauty across the table. The President and his wife wisely did not mention that they were both avid readers of Barbara Cartland novels. Weeks later, Diana would be devastated by his assassination, the first taste perhaps of the dangers of the glittering world in which she was now moving.

As soon as the Sadats departed, *Britannia* steamed down the Suez Canal and the honeymooners woke up to the sight of the old-Raj route whose shores are now littered with torn rails and over-turned tanks. As the north-bound convoy passed *Britannia,* flags were dipped and goodwill messages tapped over the air. A flotilla joined the yacht's wake as she passed into the Red Sea and a launch delivered a bouquet of roses and lilies from five Egyptian couples who had married that day.

Further south, Charles and Diana snorkled in Red Sea coral reefs and on the last night of the honeymoon, their staff staged a comedy concert. Diana played piano for a fairly bawdy singalong.

The two-week honeymoon cruise ended at Port Suez. The couple were suntanned but had been remarkably under-exposed to cameras. Such a respite would not recur for a long time.

63

SIX

Starting Work

"A woman not only marries a man, she marries
into a way of life, a job"

PRINCE CHARLES

THE Balmoral family holiday is a tradition that carries on,
romances and weddings regardless. The August–September
retreat behind the Scottish castle walls is a rare time when the
newshounds are kept at bay by an unwritten editorial word of
honour. It is a resting-up time before the busy round of official
engagements that autumn and winter bring. Diana's share of the
workload had been planned as a gentle introduction to the service
she had vowed to her country. As well as 'accompanying' (as if
she could ever be a mere accessory) the Royal Family and/or her
husband on the usual round of military inspections, walkabouts,
cross-county jaunts, premières and closings, and an opening of
Parliament, she was scheduled to tour Wales as an official co-star,
and in November to undertake her first solo engagement. Charles,
twisting his fingers no doubt with twice the normal vehemence,
would have to stay home and watch Diana on television when she
switched on Regent Street's Christmas lights.

The Princess of Wales came centre-stage at a time when the
workload on the Queen and her royal ladies was heavy. Diana has
claimed that she wants no more in life than to be a "good wife" to
Prince Charles, which of necessity means becoming an efficient
worker for the family business. As Charles in one of his most oft-
quoted statements on love and marriage said: "A woman not only
marries a man; she marries into a way of life, a job." Pregnancy
is no longer an out, as it once was for royal ladies whose
enceintement might stretch to nine months. Certainly no one
would have denied the Princess maternity leave, but though the

65

planned 1982 Commonwealth tour would have to keep and morning sickness would absent her from a few engagements, Diana stuck to her official programme even when her figure pushed her smocks to full sail. She will be a working mother for the rest of her life.

Even while still on holiday in Scotland, Diana trod gingerly into the post-nuptial public arena. One of the Palace aides told me that the Queen anticipated, and was not hurt by, the overwhelming allure of her daughter-in-law. To the reported anxiety of the Queen and the irritation of Prince Charles, Diana cut her calorie intake back to the no-breadline. At the Braemar Games, when all around her were kilted and clannish, the canny Sassenach lassie buttoned up an all-tartan Caroline Charles dress and topped it with the ultimate cliché—a tam o' shanter. Cornier, to be sure, than Glamis in August. But it knocked the Scots reeling. The games drew an unexpected crowd of ten thousand.

Becoming a Princess at the age of twenty meant putting a substantial wardrobe together quickly. She had formerly mooched around in jeans and cotton skirts and though she had a rich girl's share of 'good clothes', Diana had no need of the formal evening gowns with which her wardrobe would soon overflow. She had walked incognito into Harrods the day before her engagement and bought that sapphire Cojano suit and its pussy-cat bow blouse off the peg. For reasons best explained by several million tea caddies, she will probably never wear it again. But neither would she shop with the same unhurried ease at any store again. Even during her engagement a trip to the dressmakers meant sealing off Brook Street and placing a police cordon around Emanuels. She has bought her wardrobe piecemeal, from the school of designers rich girls can afford and of which most girls can buy reasonable imitations. Diana used to borrow T-shirts from her flat-mates; from the moment she moved into Clarence House, her sartorial mentors (except in the case of the famous black dress), were the Queen Mother and several elderly ladies in waiting. Her youngest fashion influence in this period was the efficient Mrs Shand Kydd, who whisked her daughter around Harrods and off to Bellville Sassoon to turn the formerly scruffy teenager into the toast of Buckingham Palace garden parties and Ascot. With the best intentions, though, the result was a period of bad hats and disastrous suits that featured pleats, pintucks, stripes, bows, ruffles (sometimes all on the one garment) and Queen Motherly florals. But help was at hand. Once the Princess had more time and began to trust her own intuition she became mistress of her

The Princess in her Caroline Charles outfit at the Braemar Gathering

own wardrobe, advised by several designers patronised by London's social élite. Bellville and Sassoon, the fashionable male and female team who ran up a goodly portion of the women's wear at Diana's wedding and somehow found time to make her coral honeymoon outfit, had previously proved themselves friends in need. Choosing an outfit for her betrothal pictures with the Queen was a daunting prospect for a nineteen-year-old whose previous claim to fashion note had been an unintentionally see-through skirt. But Bellville and Sassoon's most tactful sailor suit (what better to flatter a naval family?), not only won the Queen's approval but had the entire western world all at sea for a season.

With the confidence of her improving fashion record after the wedding, she chose her Welsh flag outfit off the peg from Donald Campbell's shop, appropriately called 'Chatelaine'. Her detective's approving nod sealed the deal. The Welsh would be characteristically touched at the happy combination of their

Another of John Boyd's creations—a copy of the one that topped her going-away outfit

national colours. The Princess could, of course, still wear those casual cotton prints and windbreakers of her Chelsea days. Like other members of the Royal Family, though, she has developed two wardrobes. One is for home and family, and includes her old favourites and new glamorous 'at home' clothes like the snazzy velvet evening jodhpurs she chose from Harrods in a capricious afternoon shopping session. The other 'working' wardrobe is of cocktail dresses, formal court gowns and ritzy suits for Ascot-type events. She does not regard them as her personal clothes, more public property. To wear them to a private function might be like a nurse wearing her uniform to a dinner party. But it was with this stage wardrobe that Diana needed professional help, if she was not to be dowdied by the dowagers. As both of her sisters had worked briefly for *Vogue* magazine Diana turned to this fashion bible for help. "Like any kid of nineteen," said Felicity Clark of *Vogue*, "she didn't know where to go. The idea has been to bring the best of British fashion under her eyes."

Buying almost all of designer Jasper Conran's maternity collection in one fell swoop from the fashionable Fulham Road

In fashion terms, Princess Diana towers head and shoulders over other members of the Royal Family

motherhood emporium 'Great Expectations' may have seemed an extravagance. But the dresses—which cleverly draw the eye away from the midriff with such diversions as scooped necklines —probably will not be packed away for long after the birth of the first child before being pressed back into service.

While the wardrobe grew, so did Diana's knowledge of the great expectations surrounding the behaviour of an heir's wife. Trial, error and glacial royal stares would teach her, for example, not to chatter and giggle during *God Save The Queen*. Newspaper titters guaranteed that she would only once unconsciously turn over a gift silver bowl and examine the hallmark. There were other ropes to be learned. The Queen and Queen Mother are masters of that secret royal sign language that indicates time to go (a lifting of the handbag for the Queen); ''please rescue me from this appalling bore who talks only of spaniel breeding'' (a meaningful glance to an equerry); ''I have finished eating so please do not even suggest another mouthful'' (cutlery placed diagonally across a plate). Diana had to train herself to stand for hours on end, to withstand bruised fingers from hundreds of over-eager handshakes, to develop enormous bladder capacity and to appreciate George V's advice to his sons: "Never miss an opportunity to relieve oneself as one never knows when the chance may come again." The hardest and most constant test of all, reckons Charles, is remembering never to yawn.

Times have changed since the Queen got by with a touch of mascara and a specially created lipstick called 'Balmoral' for her wedding day. Diana, who was scarcely used to applying even that, has to face harsh colour television lights every time she steps out on an official mission. If she looks pale, people will speculate that she is unwell, unhappy.

If her eyes glow like something from a cosmetic ad, people will grieve that their unspoilt Princess is turning herself into a fashionable dolly bird. Royal life is a long road of political compromise: to ensure continuity of complexion—looking neither like a washed-out Gainsborough nor Barbara Cartland's clone, the Princess early in her Buckingham Palace residence called in the £200-a-consultation expertise of Barbara Daly. Daly, who is considered Britain's top make-up artist, painted the slightly more cosmetic than normal image that stood up to the cameras of the world on the wedding day. Between them, the Princess and the cosmetologist worked out a simple routine of foundation and subtle eye-darkening that Diana can apply in a few minutes before facing cameras. She long ago gave her sandy eyelashes the brush-off with a regular tinting session at the hands of her hairdresser Kevin Shanley. Given her emotional nature and the vagaries of British weather, dyed lashes are the answer to a Princess's prayer.

Tissues are always on hand just the same. Though for the first weeks of her marriage the Princess of Wales had only the services of her maid-come-aide Evelyn Dagley, among the first appointments to the Princess's household after the honeymoon was a full-time lady in waiting. Diana had the coaching of the Queen Mother, grandmother Lady Fermoy and several Fermoy aunts who have attended royalty, for her pre-marital crash course in Palace protocol. Not having been strictly schooled from childhood like Princess Anne and other young Windsors in the Palace's mould is clearly the secret of Diana's phenomenal popularity. But with such freshness goes the inevitable case of foot-in-mouth, like the unfortunate silver bowl incident. While the public may bless her for occasional attacks of *gaucherie*, the split-second timing of her husband's schedule laments the extra five minutes of baby-kissing; hatter John Boyd grieves for the lack

Right: A posy for the Princess at Caernarvon Castle

Below: Hands reach out in St Davids

Right centre: The royal road show hits town

Right: But there were some discordant notes

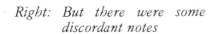

*On the first day of her Welsh tour the Princess delighted crowds by
wearing their national colours*

of millinery experience that plonks his toque on skew-whiff. Help
comes from lady in waiting Anne Beckwith-Smith, who took the
prestigious post of right-hander to the third most important lady
in the land. Prestige, fun flower shows, fascinating world tours
and the possibility of a brilliant marriage are about all Miss
Beckwith-Smith gets from the post, nevertheless. Apart from her
clothing allowance, she is unsalaried for a job which must at all
times place the Princess above her own private life. She must find
and pay for her own accommodation in London and risk disgrace
and a right royal heave-ho if an unguarded word about her
mistress passes her lips and appears in print. Not that it would, of
course. The daughter of Major Peter Beckwith-Smith (clerk of
Epsom, Sandown and Lingfield race courses) was brought up with
the type of old-school values shared by Diana herself. For her
allowance, the lady in waiting sorts Diana's mail and though she
can type, she must reply to the dozens of letters daily arriving for
her mistress. On tour with the Princess, Miss Beckwith-Smith or
one of the two part-time relief ladies must bone up on local chit-
chat. Before the Rolls pulls up in each village, the Princess must

Visiting the Royal Welsh Showground near Builth

have a dozen or so relevant items of small talk so as to strike a
chord with the local people. The lady in waiting must collect the
bouquets, the smarties and the knitted booties presented to the
Princess by waving cornfields of arms; she must hold an umbrella
over a drooping ostrich feather; help to nudge the Princess away
from those who have had their ration of small talk and keep a very
strict eye on the schedule and on her watch.

The efficiency of the system was put to the test by the first of a
lifetime of royal tours, three months after the kindergarten helper
became Princess of Wales.

The courtship and engagement were really Diana's preparations for her career in the family business. The Wales tour was her
first big assignment. Compared to some royal tours (like Charles's
five-week global trot before his wedding) Wales was a rather cushy
royal job. But it was crucial, not just for political reasons, that the
volatile Welsh should get the first visit from their Princess; the
Palace needed a short dress-rehearsal for their new recruit. Diana,
who is prone to the intense homesickness that sent her home two
terms early from her Swiss finishing school, will in the next few

years undertake long and exhausting tours to show the flag all over the world. The Wales tour—all three days and 400 miles of it—was also important to test the working of the Diana machine. On this trip, she had about eight appearances a day and two walkabouts. The royal entourage usually includes aides, ladies in waiting, a head of wardrobe, a hairdresser (though Princess Anne always styles her own hair), a secretary and the inevitable security vigilantes.

So off to Wales went the star—one of the few Princesses of Wales to set foot on Welsh soil and probably the only titleholder who has attempted to speak the language—and her roadshow. Few can have known what an emotional three days it would be for Diana. After the rest from public exposure her honeymoon and the Balmoral stay had afforded, she was back in the clicking thick of media madness and public adulation. She would be frightened by a first experience of anti-royalists protesting against her by name. She would be mobbed almost to crushing point and terrified about her speaking debut; addressed as it was to a nation which had to like her or lump her as its Princess, this first speech would be among her most important.

On top of it all, though few guessed, she was experiencing the emotional turmoil natural to any first-time mother-to-be. From behind her chic John Boyd veils, she would look at every child through new eyes; a visit to a maternity ward reduced her to fits of blushing and cooing.

The new Diana machine whirred smoothly into action. As they toured, Charles opened a map of Wales in the back seat of their Rolls-Royce. Pointing out places and airing his historical knowledge, he explained the country's past, history which is firmly intertwined with that of his—and now her—family.

As the tour began in North Wales, they swished through the same romantic countryside traversed by Madoc, Charles's mediaeval sailor ancestor. At Caernarvon, he showed her the window from which his twelfth-century ancestor was allegedly held up in his father's arms and presented to the disgruntled Welsh as their first Prince 'who could speak no English'. The Princess did not have to open her mouth to achieve her first coup. Demonstrating again her rather show-bizzy flair for achieving the desired image, she stepped out in Rhyl dressed in the Welsh national colours. Carrying a bouquet of leeks could scarcely sound more twee but the Donald Campbell outfit was in fact magnificent, right from the earlier-worn Boyd hat cleverly retrimmed in Welsh green, to her bright red Manolo Blahnik shoes. It was a hard act to

The Princess on the steps of City Hall, Cardiff

follow, particularly for a grey-suited and ever-so-slightly balding Prince. His progress through walkabout crowds had mere practice on its side: you pause at regular intervals; select a worthy face (experience has taught him to avoid pretty or over-eager young women); you ask one of about a dozen stock questions, attempt a joke at the answer and pass briskly on before the gales of nervous laughter ebb.

Observing the etiquette of keeping a few paces behind one's royal spouse is one thing. Diana lagged by a mile and had to be constantly, though unsuccessfully, hurried up. She had rejected royal tradition by refusing to shake all those cold and clammy hands with gloves for protection. ''Show us your ring, then,'' chorused the girls. She obligingly wiggled her fingers. Crowds did not hide their disappointment when it was merely the Prince of Wales, not his wife, who graced their side of the walkabouts. When the sun burst through slate skies, they attributed to Diana god-like qualities: ''Ah, she's brought us some better weather!'' A teenager presented a 'Ballad to Diana'—to Charles. He glumly conceded that he was now used to trailing along as ''a collector of flowers, these days''. Alas, he said, he did not have enough wives to go round.

75

Left: Talking to members of the choir at a Swansea concert
Right: The strain of being under the microscope sometimes shows
Opposite: The Princess's first solo engagement, switching on the
Regent Street Christmas lights

The tour was Diana's first experience of the sometimes wonderful, more often weird gifts that have by now been pressed into her hands in enough volume to start a boutique. On the same trip, she and the Prince were presented with a black Welsh heifer. Ominously, the Prince asked: ''Is she in calf?...''

The Princess is, according to the proclamation which made her a Freeman of the City of Cardiff: ''A person of distinction.'' And she is (in her own words—spoken in Welsh to the city's rapturous welcome), ''so proud to be Princess of Wales.'' If Charles was the slightest bit miffed to be sharing and for the most part missing out on much of his accustomed adulation, he was nevertheless overjoyed that the race who are inclined to treat their English Princes with hostility at the worst—ambivalence at best—were suddenly gaga about royalty. Describing the tour several days later, he formally acknowledged the source of its triumph. ''All that was entirely due to the effect that my dear wife has on everybody.''

76

SEVEN

Court Life

"It was lucky that the Spencers had such a nice coat of arms"

COLLEGE OF ARMS

THE august title 'Garter King of Arms' goes back to the 1400s, and one addresses this erudite man as "Garter". But that is the system in all its archaic oddness, the system by which a Princess who likes rock records and bubblegum will one day be attended by women of the bedchamber and a mistress of robes. The die was cast centuries ago; to update the system would mean abolishing footmen, carriages, coronations and the monarchy itself.

Lady Diana Spencer was armiginous, an apt thing for the wife of a Prince of Wales to be. It meant that she had a family coat of arms in her own right. So when the Garter King of Arms was commissioned by the Palace to produce a combined Prince and Princess of Wales coat of arms—for the first time since the 1860s—he was able to slot the neat Spencer shield (supported by a

78

manacled unicorn), beside the crest of the Prince of Wales and its attendant lion. ''It was lucky,'' a member of Garter's staff told me, ''that the Spencers had such a nice coat of arms.'' Otherwise, it could have looked a real mess. By the age of twenty, then, Diana was not just armiginous, but a co-owner of a coat of arms that might appear on some of the most prestigious crockery, stationery, flags and car pennants in the land. If she did not go to St James's that often, she lived in Kensington Palace, which has a much smarter type of neighbour. She and her husband had apartments in all the other royal castles, with office space in Buckingham Palace. The Duchy of Cornwall provided them with a nine-bedroom Georgian house in Gloucestershire, and for holidays they had a cottage in the Scilly Isles.

In the meantime, though, the normally frugal Charles was paying a high price for his long-awaited wedded bliss. Even while Diana's friends in the rag trade could get most things for her wholesale, she was reckoned to be spending over £1000 a week on clothes. It must have come as a shock to a wallet accustomed to forking out for three or four suits and a few new shirts every year. Charles had not taken a pauper for a bride. Diana had sold her London flat for a modest profit and she still had her independent Spencer income of about £10,000 a year. But a future King must support his wife in the manner to which Diana would enjoy being accustomed. Charles once prided himself on saving between ten and twenty per cent of his salary. Neither he nor his wife are on the Civil List, their income comes from the Duchy of Cornwall and from Charles's investments. But Diana and her little court—a secretary, two office girls, a maid (politely called a dresser), her shopping and the almost daily attentions of her hairdresser—must have dug into his Duchy wage at a pretty amazing rate. Three months after the wedding, he granted himself a £2500-a-week pay rise. As the workers whose pay rises were pegged to four per cent observed sourly, his was a fifty per cent increase. But the brouhaha was quickly smoothed by generous servings of Diana and, after a while, people seemed to think that £375,000 a year was a modest price to pay for a national asset with her unrationed smile and bourgeoning wardrobe.

Prince Charles, voted one of the world's best-dressed men as a toddler and one of its worst as an adult, long ago shrugged the shoulders so conservatively suited by Hawes and Curtis. ''Fashion,'' says Charles, ''by its very definition is transitory ... I dare say many of my views and beliefs would be considered old-fashioned and out of date, but that does not worry me ...'' Thus

saying, he wears the same style suits that his father and grandfather ordered. He goes off on tour with a selection which, to photographers' chagrin, all look the same. Diana, on the other hand, is delighted by her licence to be fabulously dressed and the fashion industry has become daily more royalist since the spring of 1981, when her frills accelerated the romantic revival and got the denim set into a lather of lace and ruffles.

When she was a mere royal girlfriend she was embarrassed to have her jewellery box opened by security staff at an airport. It contained a string of pearls and a few trinkets. Her watch was a big boy's model. By now her jewellery collection, largely sheikh-showered as wedding presents, has to be kept in a vault. From Saudi Arabia alone came £75,000-worth of diamonds and sapphires. If the Saudis had felt that Diana showed too much chest for Moslem modesty at King Khalid's London reception months before, they certainly gave her plenty to cover it up. Fashioned into watch bracelet, earrings and a chunky diamond pendant with a sapphire as big as a date, the collection reflected, and rather eclipsed, the design of her engagement ring. The heir apparent to Qatar presented a massive diamond collection: necklaces, a watch, bracelets and rings. The Prince and Princess of Jordan gave her an exquisite filigree choker, glittering with sapphires, rubies, emeralds and turquoises. Though Diana had worn a Spencer tiara at her wedding, the Queen's unpublicised and fabulous wedding present was an antique tiara from her own collection. It had been bequeathed by Queen Mary and worn by Queen Elizabeth many times before its giant pearl drops held by diamond love-knots came to rest on Diana's head. She wore it for the first time at her first State Opening of Parliament. For less grand occasions, she has joined the long string of royal pearl wearers, the size of her chokers having graduated from three tiers before the wedding to the great pearl collar (a wedding present from Charles) which wraps up her neck like some flamboyant vicar. She has learned to wear jewellery in much the same way as she has learned to wear hats, though newcomers to tiaras need much more than a hat pin. The hair must be threaded through the teeth of a circular comb around the tiara base; putting one on is a job for a hairdresser.

Diana's Highgrove wardrobe contains a few Chelsea relics ever ready to do royal service. Tetbury shoppers still see her striding around in jeans and a quilted body warmer as she pops into the ironmonger's. But it is the Princess's 'function' clothes, stored in her palace wardrobe, that have fashion copyists sweating over their notebooks every time she appears in public.

81

The stylish Lady Diana was the centre of attraction at Royal Ascot in 1981

Diana's clothes have always been the object of speculation, though none so great as The Dress that whispered the romance of fairy princesses with every move Diana made in St Paul's Cathedral. Within hours of the wedding ceremony, copies could be bought by brides all over the world, and a Japanese manufacturer upstaged everyone, including Diana, by producing the whole ruffled extravaganza, down to the last bow, in gold leaf. David Sassoon saw copies of the going-away suit and Mrs Shand Kydd's wedding outfit selling for a song in Marks and Spencers, and he realised that from that day the royal fashion scene would never be the same.

For the first time, the Royal Family had in their ranks a woman whose age, size, coiffure and taste reflected the mass of the market. Because she was beautiful, others wanted to look like her. Because she was wholesome, nobody's mother or husband could gripe about such imitation; suddenly it was no longer sexy to look sexy and grandmothers rejoiced that reticence was back in style, along with demure necklines and understated make-up. Because Diana achieved her 'look' with aids accessible to most working women—a well-cut hairdo, feminine clothes and hats that could be as perversely plain as a boater—her style could be adopted *en masse*. Because of who she now was, anything surprising she wore would be stamped with respectability. Thus the naughty black strapless dress got a moral uplift from a night at the opera; corny peppermint stripes and boater hats were chic after a day at the races. Uninhibited by stereotypes of which she may have simply been unaware, the Princess loved the way veils flattered her eyes and she started a collection which now includes one in most colours. Hatter John Boyd told me he keeps a special roll of silk veiling for her eyes only. It has a tiny diamond fleck and Prince Charles, says Diana, particularly likes her in it.

Few things about being royal can be unpremeditated. Even entering a room, circulating and making small talk is a studied ritual, designed to please all and be unreportable. Likewise with the wardrobe. Top echelon royal women might feel more comfortable at dinner in their corduroys, but they have a job to do, taxpayers to satisfy, and they must think of their obligations to fulfil people's fantasies every time they dress for a public event. A good proportion of Diana's expanding wardrobe is made up of function clothes, whose appearance is as much determined by the function as her own personal taste. If the Princess has, for example, to decorate an Opening of Parliament, her designer will be briefed that she must have a white gown. Because a tiara is

The Bryan Organ painting at the National Portrait Gallery—the subject of a vandal's attack

obligatory for this event, the dress must be full-length and formal; yet to be worn in daylight, it must not make the wearer look as if she's wearing a theatrical costume. As the State Opening is in early winter, the gown must have enough substance for Diana to discard her mink jacket without shivering through her mother-in-law's speech. Though it may not seem so, there are times when the Princess of Wales is very much the juvenile lead, so her gown must attempt the impossible—not to allow the young wife to outshine the Queen. "It's an extremely difficult dress to design," acknowledges David Sassoon.

There must be times for a young, easy-going Princess when climbing into another function outfit must be as welcome as a strait-jacket. But royal ladies have much in common with actresses or film stars. Though most clothes are prudently selected with the knowledge that form must fit function, some of Diana's most surprising and successful outfits have been bought on impulse. She wafted into Bellville Sassoon one day to supervise the making of her working gear and spied the designers' sketches for a Russian-style collection for the following season. She left having ordered an Anna Karenina ensemble, hat (lamb's-wool done out as astrakhan) and at David Sassoon's persuasion, a giant muff. The outfit's success (fittingly on the coldest day for years), was probably enough to assure Bellville and Sassoon of the success of their future collection—even though every Tom, Dick and Harry in the rag trade might have copied the look before the month was out.

When Diana arrives at Buckingham Palace for a day at the office, she may meet the Queen in the corridor and make her morning curtsey in dungarees. Life within the Palace nevertheless has the business etiquette of any great family company. The Queen, for example, would never drop in on her executive son in his office or apartment without first buzzing a warning and Diana cannot visit any of her royal relatives without first checking that the moment is convenient. She calls most of them by their first names and they, even the children, call her Diana. She is formally addressed by her staff and the public as "Your Highness" or "Ma'am", though the absent-minded are not reproached for letting the odd "Lady Diana" slip. Close friends from pre-royal days, including her hairdresser, may lapse into the familiar "Diana" in private. The Queen is one of the first monarchs to abolish bowing and curtseying by her children at every meeting and only on formal, public occasions would Diana expect a curtsey from a subordinate member of the Royal Family, or from her own family and friends. Though one should make a quick bob or neck-bow when presented to the Princess of Wales, she would never expect genuflexions from anyone she singled out for a chat in a walkabout crowd.

There is no escaping the fact, however, that as Princess of Wales, people are starting to think of her as their someday Queen and treating this former child-minder with reverence that still

The Princess now appears on the stamps of seventeen
Commonwealth countries (see p. 128)

staggers her. Included in the mail that floods her desk every day are suggestions that she becomes Colonel-in-Chief of military regiments (she is expected to take command of the 13/18 Hussars of Light Brigade fame) and hundreds of requests for her to be patron of charitable organisations. Here she takes ministerial advice before deciding which to accept. Her husband has more than 300 patronages and is Colonel-in-Chief of nine regiments, but Diana's child-rearing commitments will prevent such formidable public duties. Her sister-in-law's affiliations may provide a more realistic guide; Princess Anne is Colonel-in-Chief of nine regiments, Chancellor of London University and lends her name to medical projects such as breast-cancer research. She is President of the Save the Children Fund and the British Academy of Film and Television Arts and patron of the Riding for the Disabled Association and the Jersey Wildlife Preservation group. She also likes to accept invitations to events near her home in Gloucestershire. Diana's early choices for personal charities included four children's organisations. She is patron of the Pre-school Playgroups Association, the Malcolm Sargent Cancer Fund for children, the Royal School for the Blind and the Albany Community Centre—a South-East London group which deals with children at risk.

Tactfully, she also accepted the role of prima patron of the Welsh National Opera.

Diana's engagements are fairly rigidly set six months ahead, for each royal household has two planning meetings a year to fix its calendar. Charles and Diana sit in on each other's meetings and decide which functions they will attend together. Planning meetings are long and drawn out, full of 'ums' and 'ahs', leafing through diaries and almost comic royal balancing acts. There are, Charles might say, too many hospital visits in July—what about a school or a drainage plant? A corset factory? Marvellous. Venues are crucial; the Royal Family like to spread themselves around geographically and it is politic to appear as often in, say, Brixton as in more up-market spots.

On Diana's desk are regular requests to name things after her. Pubs are flatly refused permission but libraries, schools or other 'suitable' institutions consult the Home Office for approval. A Princess of Wales hospital wing in Australia was the first institution legitimately to take her name, just months after the wedding. She gets hundreds of requests for autographed pictures, to which her staff reply with a gentle 'No'. Diana reads only a small proportion of her mail. Most replies are drafted in handwriting and signed by her secretary or lady in waiting. She never dictates letters. Only correspondence of a personal nature, like thank-you notes, is written in her small, backward-sloping hand. She does not enjoy letter-writing but practice makes perfect: during the Balmoral leg of the honeymoon, Diana joined Charles in writing 1250 thank-you letters to the tenants in the Duchy of Cornwall who had subscribed to their wedding present.

Speeches are an occupational hazard enjoyed by Charles and his father but few other members of the Royal Family. Diana will be obliged to make more as she becomes less of an accessory to her husband and takes on more solo engagements. Her secretary does the research and prepares a draft but the words delivered are her own. At the end of a working day, Diana will drive herself back to Kensington Palace, the new London residence of the Prince and Princess of Wales. Their wing has just undergone a £750,000 refit, largely at the expense of the Department of the Environment.

Pupils at Dick Sheppard School, Tulse Hill, greeting the Princess who helps with a fund-raising campaign

But the couple may need to hang a 'bless this home' sign over the mantle, for calamities started striking here long before World War II bombs fell. The Wren-repaired palace has been dubbed 'hoodoo house' by generations of royalty. William II bought it, lock, stock and gargoyle, for £20,000. Before he moved in, part of the building fell down, narrowly missing Queen Mary and killing several householders. As soon as the couple settled in, fire broke out and the King was lucky to escape in his nightshirt. Mary died of smallpox there some years later and William died in agony in his palace bed after an equestrian accident. Queen Anne happily introduced 'KP' to her consort, George of Denmark, in 1703 and tended his deathbed there six years later—five years before her own demise. In 1760 George II passed away there after a breakfast of mutton chops, kidneys, kippers and oysters. His ghost is said to haunt the window of the room where he died to this day. Royal marriages have blown on to the rocks here, including those of the Regent George and Caroline of Brunswick and Princess Margaret and Lord Snowdon. Margaret now lives at this desirable, but

87

Kensington Palace, the London home of the Prince and Princess

jinxed, address with happier neighbours; the Duke and Duchess of Gloucester and Prince and Princess Michael of Kent.

Diana's father, wracking his brains before Christmas for a present suitable for the Princess of Wales, said: "I suppose you could describe her as the girl who has everything." Yet in becoming one of the most privileged people alive, Diana gave up many everyday human rights. Legally, she can still vote but to preserve the political non-alignment of the Royal Family, she probably never will again. In an age where fortunes can be made by confidantes confiding to the mass media, she will guard her tongue and be forced to talk trivia in all but the most private conversations. She can never explode with rage or write to *The Times* on an issue of controversy, indeed she will be discouraged from feeling strongly about anything. During the royal busy season, she will be separated from her husband for days on end—weeks, if pregnancies preclude her accompanying him on overseas trips. She can never get up and leave when an event is so stultifyingly dull that she must concentrate hard to stop her jaws from yawning. Unlike Caroline of Brunswick, a former Princess of Wales, who suffered the company of bores only to exclaim afterwards: "Mein Gott, dat is de dullest person Gott Almighty ever did born," Diana will be publicly fascinated by bores and professionally polite with people she cannot stand.

A contemplative Diana, strolling alone in London the day before her engagement was announced

She sits down to banquets when she feels like baked beans. But she does have the final say on what she eats. If she is watching her weight, she can set a calorie limit on the meal. She will go nowhere without her own bottled drinking water as a safeguard against tummy bugs and she will prefer the Malvern brand for its non-aeration. Diana might stay home from an event where she was merely accompanying Charles if she has morning sickness. But if she has undertaken an engagement in her own right, the show must go on. A day's programme in the early months of her first pregnancy started at 9.23 am, when she stepped from the royal train at York, shook hands with a dozen dignitaries and left for a railway museum. At 10.45 am, she and Charles shook a few hundred hands on a short walkabout. By 11 am, they were on their way by helicopter to Chesterfield, where Diana shook a few dozen more hands and unveiled an inscription. They then visited the town's information centre and at 2.45 pm, shook scores of policemen's hands when they opened the new divisional headquarters. At 3.20 pm, they were delivered to their helicopter and flown to Sandringham.

Diana herself describes the job as ''thirty per cent fantastic and seventy per cent sheer slog''. Having a baby is a brief hiatus; work can begin again for royal mothers as little as eight weeks after delivery.

EIGHT

An Heir

THE Queen was touring New Zealand when, at a lavish Polynesian festival, something happened that might be interpreted as the first clue that the patter of little heirs might soon be heard in Kensington Palace. For Polynesians, children give *mana* to a family. The first son automatically inherits the family's right to be heard as a political voice. This son is called the *Tuakana* and he should traditionally be produced as soon as possible after marriage. The Maoris, with whom Charles had pressed noses on his 1981 New Zealand tour, call the Queen's eldest son 'the *Tuakana* of the Commonwealth'. So when Graham Latimer, the president of the Maori Council, addressed the Queen and the Duke just two and a half weeks before Diana's pregnancy was announced, his comments were polite by Maori tradition—even if their familiarity staggered the British press. Latimer, a dairy farmer, told the Queen he had heard rumours that she might soon become a grandmother again. "If that is not true," he added soberly, "then the message I have for you is to tell Prince Charles to get on with the job."

The gasp from British writers was followed by another surprise. A majestic glacial stare usually indicates when a remark offends. But the Queen and the Duke had their heads back, laughing. Perhaps they knew how true were the words. Certainly, back in Scotland, Charles and Diana must have had their suspicions. Only days before Latimer's remarks, Diana had taken unscheduled leave from post-honeymoon holidays and flown to London on a commercial flight. 'Shopping' was the reason given officially, though subsequent sleuthing put one and one together and came up with three. George Pinker, the Queen's gynaecologist, had been in London and even though the pregnancy can have been only weeks on at the time, very modern ultra-sonic scanning techniques can provide clues at such an early stage. With Diana's heavy programme of engagements in the New Year, not to mention a skiing holiday, the couple would have needed confirmation as soon as possible.

The Queen and Duke were in Australia during these exciting events but their daily telephone calls home might have ferreted out Charles and Diana's glad suspicions. There was absolutely no mistaking their amusement at Latimer's bold joke and the Polynesians heard it as a logical enough sentiment: ''It's quite traditional to tell a couple to hurry it up in producing their first child—the *tuakana*,'' Latimer told me.

Unnecessary in this couple's case though; Charles and Diana had already hurried up one of the faster pregnancies in recent royal history. And on their Wales trip about two weeks later, they were handing out wholesale hints of their own, almost challenging the public to speculate. The Princess had skipped, Cinderella-fashion, home from evening engagements soon after nine. While only Diana was expected to inspect a maternity wing in Tonypandy, both husband and wife had charged into the baby-zone with unconcealed enthusiasm. Diana was even heard to squeal ''babies!'' as she swept through the swing doors, pouncing on a new mother and grilling her for details . . . ''how long were you in labour . . . and what was it like?'' Soon after his brother-in-law Mark Phillips had been the first husband present at a royal birth, Prince Charles slapped the Wales seal of approval on paternal involvement. Taking on his occasional self-appointed-expert air, he pronounced: ''I think it is a very good thing for the husband to be with the mother when she is having their baby.'' *Sotto voce* he added, ''I expect I shall get a lot of letters about this.'' Welsh nurses clucked knowingly and said (after the announcement a few days later) that yes, she did have that early-pregnancy bloom about her.

The announcement, itself a sign of the royal times, came aptly enough on November 5, Guy Fawkes Day. Only in recent years has it been Palace etiquette to announce anything as intimate as the delicate state of royal ladies so soon or in such frank terms. In the era of the Queen's pregnancies, there might be speculation when Princess Elizabeth took a chair to watch a military display—something unheard of among the upright Windsors who

The ladies in waiting, Anne Beckwith-Smith, Hazel West and Lavinia Baring

are trained from infancy to stand through a blizzard—but no early announcements. After about the fourth month, a rather stuffy notice that ''the Princess would undertake no further engagements'' would provide cause for much public rejoicing and counting on fingers. In the case of the ninth Princess of Wales, Buckingham Palace simply said: ''The Princess of Wales is expecting a baby next June.''

Both families were delighted, continued the notice; the Queen was informed some days before; Mrs Shand Kydd was ''absolutely overjoyed''; the Princess hoped to continue public engagements but regretted any curtailments in her planned programme; she would be attended by George Pinker, surgeon-gynaecologist to the Queen.

No one who knew Diana seemed surprised at the speed with which she started her family. Lifelong friend Teresa Mowbray predicted at the time of the engagement that: ''Lady Diana will have children very quickly . . . she simply adores children . . . I would think she would want to start a family as soon as possible.'' Buckingham Palace was clearly not party to such gems of prophecy. It was already arranging a Commonwealth tour—a nightmare of advance planning which is never undertaken just for the thrill of cancellation—and even the Prince did not foresee such instant fatherhood. He told me before his wedding that he hoped to return to the South Pacific with his wife-to-be in the ''near future''. Ironically, on the day his engagement was hastily

93

announced as a rearguard action against a massive press leak, the Prince's busy work schedule had to be aborted and he had laughed: ''I have always wanted to throw a spanner in the works of my programme; I think I have managed to throw in a crow-bar.'' Ten months later, with his ''dear wife'', he had managed to repeat the feat with spanners, crow-bars a gross of baby rattles, and a dose of morning sickness: not that he or anyone else was complaining.

The couple rode the gauntlet of public curiosity soon after the news had been announced and endured thousands of eyes on Diana's waist. She took lunch at the Guildhall with a creditable attempt at indifference and smiled politely at the inevitable rush-job line from the Lord Mayor, Col Sir Ronald Gardner Thorpe, to the effect that babies were ''stardust blown from the hands of God''. Even Charles effected a little over-zealous paternalism by rushing to help her with a coat which she had hitherto been able to manage unaided. The radio announcement seemed to have changed the sylph-like Diana, who only the evening before had worn a frothy, off-the-shoulder gown, displaying a 22-inch waist, into the mother-to-be in a huge woollen coat that could contain a nine-month bulge; and aptly, she was tucking zestfully into a three-course meal (eating for at least two) and telling the chef how yummy it was. Dramatically speaking, she was hamming it up irresistibly and proving that the logical progression from all the world loving a lover, was for all the world to cluck rapturously and love a mum.

No one more than the Welsh. Still glowing from the radiant progress of a long-awaited Princess through their valleys, they now had a Wales junior to look forward to. The combination of bonfire night with the happy nappy news had a rash of celebrations breaking out nationally. Great Brington, Diana's home village, rolled out the barrel with *cuvée* left over from the wedding day at lunch time and was in a euphoric haze by tea. Tetbury, whose rockets were soaring up in sight of Highgrove's nursery (among the first of the rooms redecorated by Dudley Poplak), broke out the champagne. ''It would be marvellous,'' said the mayor of a town whose property values had rocketed since the new neighbours arrived, ''if she gave birth at Highgrove . . . but of course that's up to her.''

Politically, just like the engagement, the pregnancy announcement was opportune. To anti-monarchist MP Willie Hamilton, a royal wedding meant Britain was in for ''six months of mush'' which would take the emphasis off what his party saw as

The Princess's first day on the visit to her Principality

Margaret Thatcher's industrial and economic mismanagement. Just the day before Diana's pregnancy was announced, Premier Thatcher had staked her reputation on putting Britain right in one year—a grim last gambit to ensure her survival as Prime Minister in a country with the greatest unemployment total since the Great Depression. The ''six months of mush'' that began with cheering Londoners outside the Palace the next morning must have been music to her ears.

The pregnancy was good for business in general. Lyn Hooper, the Leeds Diana-lookalike who earns a living imitating the

95

Princess, could not believe her luck. The Di-clone had discoverd herself pregnant a few weeks before and thought herself all washed up. "I'll be in demand right up to the birth and after," she calculated, posing with a carrycot. Diana had been good for fashion ever since she sashayed into a salmon stream in knickerbockers. Her pregnant pause was seen as another shot in the arm for the rag trade as maternity gear stepped proudly out of the closet.

"A marriage is not only for the two people who are forming the marriage," Charles once said. "It is also for the children." By the age of 33 he had been godfather to a great gaggle of well-bred British children. His own child was sorely wanted for emotional as well as dynastic reasons. If the speed with which Diana obliged left him a little shell-shocked, the Prince quickly fell into the role he enjoys most, being authoritative. Days after the announcement, when Diana started a particularly miserable period of morning sickness and had to call off a series of engagements, he liked to assure reporters: "You've all got wives, you know the problems . . . it's better not to do too many things." At a corset factory, where the staff's faces were drawn in with disappointment at the absence of the Princess, he nodded sagely, "After about three months, things are inclined to get better." Rather

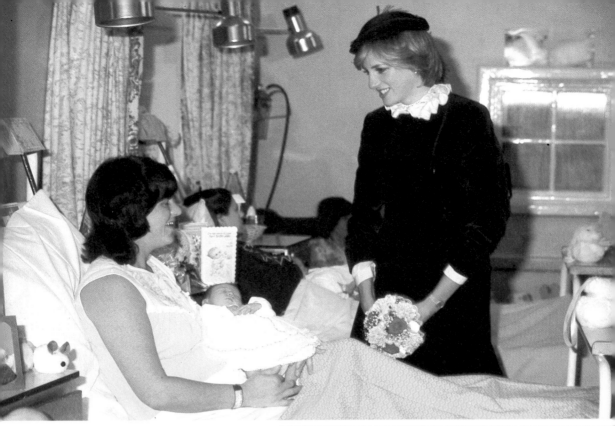

Delight and enthusiasm in the maternity ward in Llwynypia Hospital

But her pregnancy was not obvious at the opening of the Gonzaga exhibition, the night before the announcement

Opposite: The Royal Family, an impressive phalanx, on the steps of St George's Chapel, Windsor, at Christmas

chauvinistically he added, ''I am prepared to take full responsibility.'' The mother-to-be was rather more open about her ignorance, ever aware that her style of naïvety engendered only greater adoration. Despite the expertise of her gynaecologist, George Pinker, she was obviously missing the support of others in the same predicament as herself. ''Nobody told me I would feel like this,'' she lamented to all and sundry as the nausea struck. She grabbed the hands of another mother-to-be in Derbyshire and talked about her agony. ''Oh, that morning sickness, isn't it dreadful!''

George Pinker probably had the same advice for this patient as for any of his other mothers-to-be: ''Lead as normal a life as possible without indulging in excesses, neither eating for two nor walking two miles a day if you are not used to it; get yourself informed about the changes that occur during pregnancy and accept modern help.'' Pinker's 'modern help', the best that money can buy, is offered in the private Lindo Wing of St Mary's Hospital, Paddington. How different from Charles's own birth. As Princess Elizabeth went into labour in Buckingham Palace in 1948, the Duke of Edinburgh played squash to let off steam. But the Queen's gynaecologist favours Charles's method of wife-support. The husband's presence at the birth, he says, ''helps the mother very much. I also think it strengthens the bond between them.'' Chief among Diana's little helpers during her pregnancy have been Chinese bees. She took a three-month course in Royal Jelly capsules, whose contents include wheatgerm and the honey from hives in China. The jelly is said to balance a pregnant woman's system, improve her hair and skin and give her plenty of energy. After all, the bees feed it to the queen bee to enable her to lay up to 2000 eggs a day. Charles made sure Diana had plenty of rest, even if his dragging Diana out on long pheasant shoots caused a rather public row between the two and a national tut-tutting in Diana's sympathy. Though their skiing break—a traditional January pilgrimage by Charles to the Klosters resort—had to be cancelled, the couple escaped to the remote Caribbean island of Windermere for over a week in February to get away from it all. Or that was the intention. Jetting after them, hiring yachts to circle the virtually inaccessible isle, was the Fleet Street fleet.

Pictures of a slightly bulbous Diana in a strapless bikini were splashed over two national tabloids within a day of the couple's arrival at Windermere. The Queen was furious. The public jammed the Palace telephone lines in outrage. The *Sun* said: ''The pictures were carefree, innocent and delightful. They

Princess Anne: ''It is Charles and Diana's turn now''

brought a breath of summer into the lives of millions of our readers . . . of course it was never our intention to offend . . . if we have done so, then we are deeply sorry.'' They were in fact so sorry that they published the bikini shot again with the apology.

The Princess was set up in her own chintzy sitting-room office on the second floor of Buckingham Palace, overlooking a wintry Mall where she had driven as the whole world's dream summer bride, half a year and a half a world ago. After breakfast—which she now ate—she and Charles would leave their temporary and rather cramped Palace apartment and go to their adjacent offices. For Diana, the mail came in volume that varied from a dozen to a hundred letters a day; from children, the elderly and from organisations that wanted her professional services as an opener, closer or attender. With a neat little bow from the neck, secretary Oliver Everett would place the letters that needed her personal attention on her blotter. Notes from friends would be especially marked and presented unopened. So work went on until the final stages of her pregnancy.

NINE

Private Life

"There are very few people I know to whom I could speak with any degree of freedom"

PRINCESS ANNE

THE Princess of Wales liked to take a cottage in Bayswater where she spent whole days under an assumed name, pretending to be an ordinary person. It was easier for Caroline of Brunswick. There were no television, no cameras and no superstar syndrome in the early 1800s and though royal figures were often caricatured, few ordinary Londoners would recognise them if they stepped out without their fine clothes and fancy entourages. In 1982 the Princess of Wales went to Harrods, her old pre-marital shopping ground. None of the flashing demon *paparazzi* was in sight. Nevertheless, shoppers and tourists recognised Diana, as instantly as if she had been Bardot at St Tropez. She was mobbed. The hands reached to touch, the pocket instamatics clicked. Her detective saw the terrified look in her eyes and moved to herd the sightseers away.

During a school visit in Brixton, the much-maligned press (with the exception of a small official rota) was locked outside the school grounds. Yet inside the school, where Diana circulated among pupils and school officials, invited guests stood on chairs taking pictures. Polaroid may be a wonder of science, but it has not improved anyone's manners. She might be talking to someone even as they snapped and flashed and the muzzy image of herself appeared a foot from her eyes. Neither is rubber-necking confined to the suburbs. At the State Opening of Parliament, peers and their jewelled ladies craned their necks and squinted lorgnetted eyes during the largely unnoticed speech by the Queen. Diana was the focus, in her 'new' Queen Mary tiara. Charles, hand chivalrously on his sword, cast black looks (also unnoticed) at the

101

Diana at Broadlands with her friend Lady Romsey

galleries. Few would know before the next day, but Diana was pregnant and feeling phased and vulnerable under the relentless X-ray eye of the public.

Weeks after her pregnancy was announced, an unprecedented meeting was held at Buckingham Palace. The Palace invited newspaper, broadcasting and press association editors to meet with press secretary Michael Shea. He launched an extraordinary appeal: please give the Princess a break. She was, explained Shea, under ''great strain'' because of the constant presence of cameras at every juncture of her life. Even at Highgrove, her home, she felt she ''could not go out of her front door without being photographed''. After half an hour thus lectured, the gentlemen of the press stepped through to an adjoining room, where they were surprised to find the Queen. She offered them drinks and, when questioned off the record, she confirmed her anxiety and added a personal plea for Diana's privacy.

Prince Charles had ended his honeymoon press session at Balmoral by wishing news-gatherers a happy Christmas—his tactful, if naïve suggestion being that Fleet Street and the Prince and Princess of Wales might happily exist without each other for a while. Sure enough, interest in Charles curtailed obligingly. But the Princess was proving to be a royal ornament no one could afford to ignore. But following the announcement of her pregnancy and the epidemic-level interest in Diana, there was a rash of cancellations on her part. Some felt it was not just morning sickness, especially since nausea had not prevented her following the guns over arduous miles on one of Charles's pheasant shoots. The suggestion was that the real ailment was the strain of too many eyes and too many cameras. Not just from the scapegoat press. Diana-gawping was the latest spectator sport wherever she went. On official podia, top brass would stare fixedly at her. Something sinister was also happening to her private life, too. It was disappearing. Being Princess of Wales, she discovered, was a profession from which one could never clock off.

Charles had bought Highgrove, their Gloucestershire seat, with her approval before the engagement. The sweethearts had not realised that the estate's low walls, public thoroughfares (now blocked) and the close proximity of a road—not to mention the Princess-mania about to sweep Europe—would turn their happy home into a tourist attraction to rival Presley's Gracelands. It was not something their new gate, a present from the hospitable villagers of nearby Tetbury, could lock out. The local hotel's ten rooms had been booked solid with British, French, German

Highgrove House

and North American photographers since the baby news. A French magazine operated a photographic shift system outside Highgrove. (When the German magazines could not get a picture, they faked it. One cover had Diana's head pasted on the body of a woman holding a puppy, with the Queen Mother smiling benignly into the collage. 'She gave Diana a little dog so the baby could have a playmate,' fantasised the caption.) Brazil had used Diana's face to advertise soap powder and razor blades. The Britons had not been playing much cricket, either. Pictures of the Prince and Princess kissing and dancing in gum-boots on their lawn were shot by a freelance photographer who happened to be passing the house at the time, in much the same manner as he had been passing it for days on end. For all their unfocused fuzziness, they were splashed on front pages. Everytime Diana went on her wine gum and chocolate expeditions to Tetbury, cameras followed. Every item she bought, and its cost, was solemnly reported.

The implication was that the gum-boot, wine and bubblegum habits of this twenty-year-old were not in line with the image of a future Queen. Probably, Diana felt she was no longer free to be herself, the self everyone had found so endearing in the first place. The Queen acted. The editors were chastened. In a leader title ''The Captive Princess'', *The Times* described Diana as ''snapped and pinned like an errant butterfly to the front pages of

103

various prints'' in her private moments. ''The idea that the Princess might send a servant for the wine gums is pompous if not preposterous. It would be nice to think we are grown up enough not to imprison a Princess in a palace.''

''There are very few people I know to whom I could speak with any degree of freedom,'' Princess Anne once said. Palace walls tend to have ears. The day is gone when the vocation of serving royalty was passed jealously from father to son and virtue was its own reward. Front-page revelations from former servants have embarrassed the Royal Family over the past few years. For money considerably greater than their wages, they have revealed the Queen's and Duke's eating patterns—from the brand of biscuit Her Majesty munches with her pre-breakfast cuppa, to her strangely possessive habits with chocolate cake. Diana had her first taste of staff indiscretion when Charles's valet, one of the longest stayers in his household, packed his bags and told newspapers of clashes between himself and the Princess over Charles's clothing. The family are not big spenders in any department, least of all servants' wages. When Charles and Diana wanted a cook for Highgrove, Palace chefs turned up their noses at the cheese-paring wages. The couple had to advertise decorously in *The Lady.* ''Everyone who applies for a job is vetted very

Above: With the Royal Family on Buckingham Palace balcony

Opposite: In the royal box at Smith's Lawn

Right: With Prince Edward at Christmas

closely, almost from the cradle,'' says the Queen's press secretary. ''Everyone is given elaborate checkouts.'' Staff are expected to sign certain agreements, which probably specify not talking to the press.

Rosanna Lloyd, of good Welsh family and no doubt a whiz at Charles's favourite scrambled eggs, got the cullinery job. Starting what promises to be a successful royal career, she said she was ''honoured to be chosen'', and nothing more. There is a tacit gentlepersons' agreement between Diana and the people who serve her and wish to do so for long enough to land a royal warrant when she starts dispensing them. As milliner John Boyd says, ''it gives you a handle to your jug''. But you handle it with care. Kevin Shanley, Diana's hairdresser of five years' standing, sitting and now flying to Balmoral for stylings, enjoys the publicity of this post and gives interviews. They are, however, largely exercises in frustration, for though he will praise her beauty to the heavens, he is hellishly cagey about something as obvious and tangible as her post-marital weight-loss. ''Personally, I never noticed,'' Shanley says blandly. ''There's no agreement between the Princess and I. I get asked a lot of questions and if there's something I don't want to answer, I won't.'' Says designer David Sassoon: ''You are discreet or they would not come to you. Their clothes are a personal thing. It's rather like being a doctor—very difficult at times.'' Royal relatives, who would not thank me for using their names, say that to err slightly in discretion will be recognised as human in tradespeople. But silence is most uncompromisingly expected from relatives.

One thing that anybody who wishes to remain in Diana's service will never discuss is her mode of coming and going and the security involved. But clients at the hatter's, the dress shop and the crimper's (where Diana still sometimes goes to have her hair done) will see Diana's personal detective Graham Smith sitting, sipping coffee, in a perfumed environment which makes a change from the horsey aromas that came as part of the work for his former boss Princess Anne. Smith is sandy, handsome, 40ish, married and a snappy dresser. He is good company for Diana with his engaging dinner-table repartee and his fashion sense (he gave the casting nod to her red and green Wales outfit) and as one who has had the pleasure, I can say he is a great dancer. Service to female royal households has taught him infinite patience. They also serve who sit and wait in hairdressers for hours.

Within Palace walls, Diana's little 'court' comprises people in whom she can confide without fear of leaks. Beyond suspicion is

Prince Charles is godfather to the son of his great friends Lord and Lady Tryon

Oliver Everett, her polo-playing secretary. He saved Charles's life after a polo match in Florida; the Prince collapsed from heat exhaustion and Everett applied cold towels and rushed the Prince to hospital. Here the aide allegedly heard the immortal lines: ''Don't leave me, Oliver, I think I'm going to die.'' Naturally, Everett is too discreet to confirm this. Diana's lady in waiting, Anne Beckwith-Smith, stands firm through fair and foul weather, warding off the occasional bores which are a royal occupational hazard. Her presence proves her loyalty; she is not paid a penny. Evelyn Dagley's humour and discretion as Diana's maid was proved on the honeymoon, after which Fleet Street would have given its drinking arm for details. On the final night, she

The Princess and her entourage arrive at Brixton

entertained the Prince and Princess by dressing in a bikini and joining two detectives in a parody of *We are Sailing*. Diana shares the unflinching loyalty of Charles's courtiers, including former libel lawyer Edward Adeane (the Prince's private secretary) and assistant private secretary Francis Cornish, whose accent is pure BBC but whose humour has the wryness of Cornwall. Cornish can swear like a trooper but, like his boss, never in front of the Princess. Diana does not swear and her blasphemies are limited to the occasional "Oh, God".

Among the few with whom Diana need not watch her tongue is former flatmate Anne Bolton. Along with the other two friends of the Colherne Court days, Anne was among the first to know—and the last to admit knowledge of—Diana's engagement. This loyal silence continued when the Princess called secretly with news of her pregnancy. Anne, an Oxford brigadier's daughter, has been invited to Balmoral and sometimes has received surprise visits from Diana at the Mayfair estate agency where she works. As Charles's former valet Stephen Barry sadly observed, some people's values are distorted by the fact that one is a confidant of royalty. "It's like the song *I danced with a boy who danced with a*

Right: A bouquet from a shy young man in Hyde Park

Below: At a carol service in Guildford Cathedral

girl who danced with the Prince of Wales—everybody is interested in me only because I dressed the future King of England.'' Anne Bolton told me: ''We get asked a lot of things. There are no rules. We don't talk about any of our friends. Why should we talk about Diana?''

Back at Tetbury, the couple are ''more regular church-goers than some of the locals,'' says the vicar of St Mary's, Michael Sherwood. On some Sundays when they are in residence, they telephone the vicar and he secretly saves them a seat in the front row. They arrive dead on time, sing along with the hymns, put a pound note in the plate and go home, usually dodging the ritual helloing and handshaking afterwards. Highgrove occupants have an historical connection with the church. In 1890 St Mary's tower was rebuilt by the house's owners on the understanding that nothing would be allowed to impede their view of such philanthropy. To this day, no buildings or trees have been allowed to block their view, a tradition which Charles may well curse, for it makes his house one of the most exposed in town. Some drivers, astonished at Highgrove's visibility, have screeched to a halt on the road outside and caused accidents.

Tetbury, a grey stone and slate town bypassed by the A433 and the industrial revolution, found overnight in 1980 that there was more to prosperity than a full woolsack. When a 31-year-old bachelor paid £800,000 for the house and 346-acre estate called Highgrove, then announced his engagement six months later, Tetbury discovered tourism. High society discovered Tetbury and moved in *en masse*; property values rose ten per cent in a year. The mayor, antique dealer Brian Kimber, stopped being cut up about how thin on the ground his cherished oak chairs were. Local business had perked up through another aristocratic seat. He was slow to admit that Charles and Diana were the best thing that ever happened to Tetbury. ''But yes, they are,'' he agreed reluctantly. Kimber breeds cavalier King Charles spaniels, chairs the local Conservative Party branch and is logically a keen royalist. So is the town. It has welcomed Princess Anne and her husband to nearby Gatcombe Park, Prince and Princess Michael of Kent to Nether Lypiatt Manor, a host of horsey royalty to the local Beaufort Hunt and to the nearby Badminton horse trials. Charles and Diana were as welcome as the first cuckoos, though the inevitable influx of cameras and notebooks has worn thin in its novelty. ''We've not cashed in commercially,'' Mayor Kimber told me. ''That's not the sort of people we are. We like to think that members of the Royal Family have been able to come

King Olav, Diana, Princess Alice and the Queen Mother at the Remembrance Day service

here—and will continue to do so—without undue harassment.'' High hopes. But royal neighbours can also be taxing for the locals at times. To keep a police vigil on Highgrove is costing ratepayers about £50,000 a year. Princess Anne's presence costs them £30,000 and the Kents' lilliputian Lypiatt needs a mere £20,000 contribution from locals. If residents in the Gloucestershire–Wiltshire triangle are pleased about their new neighbours, the feeling should be mutual.

Charles and Diana have their own burglar alarm system inside Highgrove House. The couple's detectives are always on hand and, during Dudley Poplak's £250,000 renovations to the Georgian house, local workmen were asked to install a steel lining for a first-floor bathroom. More romantically, one of Highgrove's 30 or more rooms has been lined with Harris tweed; at £6 a yard a very un-Scots-like reminder of Scotland. In the large, blue and gold nursery is the canopied hand-me-down royal cradle. It held Charles and all the Queen's babies before getting a retrim in expectation of Diana's first child. Although Diana has a housekeeper-cook, three maids, a butler, three footmen and can call on extras from Buckingham Palace if she needs rein-

111

The fairy-tale Princess on her way to the Opening of Parliament

forcements for a big party at Highgrove, she is personally involved in the running of her own home. She likes to cook—a Russian borsch is among her favourite recipes—and those who have tasted her efforts at barbecuing disagree with her insistence that she is an "only average" cook. She demonstrated her practicality and determination to establish a functional kitchen in the way she controlled, to a certain extent, the nature of her wedding presents. Neither was Charles joking when he talked about "camping on my orange boxes" at Highgrove. As a bachelor, he barely had an egg whisk to bless himself. Diana, deciding to be the first royal wife to get what she actually needed, made a successful bid to channel the orgy of wedding gift-giving in a direction that would equip two empty homes. High society raised a high brow when Diana registered her list at the General Trading Company in London. It included sauté pans, omelette pans, casseroles, salt and pepper mills, champagne and highball glasses. Her practicality paid off. On her wedding eve, she declared the controversial list idea a success. ''It's all come to us, it's marvellous.'' But 22 toasters, Ma'am? ''We have got two houses to fill.''

As it turned out, the couple could have filled two museums with the treasures they collected. Valued at £5 million, the presents and the wedding dress—which in its glass case assumed the mysticism of a shapely shroud of Turin—drew queues over a mile long when it went on display in St James's Palace after the wedding. For Diana's kitchens came microwave ovens, bread-boards, blenders, spice racks and recipe books. To nurse a fallen horseman, she got a first-aid kit. There was a surfeit of double beds and furnishings for every room of every house they might care to live in; for the outdoors came garden seats, twin hammocks and planters. No cup of Prince of Wales tea need ever go cold with the tea cosies cast on in bulk by British knitters. Saucepans and treasures alike were packed up by a team of removal experts and freighted in convoy to Highgrove several months later.

It soon became apparent that what had seemed like a spacious house for two was a cramped house for the couple's wedding presents, their staff and attendant security men. If Diana was serious about having ''lots and lots of children'', she may be house-hunting before long.

Not that they are short of a palace. Their wing of Kensington Palace aside, annual migrations will see Charles and Diana in castles and royal houses all over Britain, for the traditional holidays which offer more privacy than royal Tetbury can provide. Strolling kilted in the heather, Charles is wont to declare Balmoral ''the best place in the world to be''. It is among the most private for a Prince and Princess of Wales when they retreat to the Scottish castle for about a month every autumn with the immediate Royal Family; there exists an *entente cordiale* between Queen and media that Balmoral is no pressman's land. The locals have been clannish with the Royal Family ever since John Brown and ''that wee German lady'', Queen Victoria, roamed the glens. Ballater shopkeepers, who may be quizzed by press outriders about what the low-key majesty in a Land Rover came to the village for, are apt suddenly to have no recall of the lady. Here, many of the shops are Royal Warrant holders and likely to remain

Prince Charles leaves Heathrow for President Sadat's funeral

so. Generations of shopkeepers have learned to make no fuss if a
Queen or a Princess ambles in, so Diana and Sarah Armstrong-
Jones, out shopping together, provoke no more comment than,
''Wha' can I do for ye two wee lassies?'' Some days the younger

royal set at Balmoral removes itself to the Queen Mother's most un-dowagerish dower house, Birkhall. Some nights, Sarah and Diana join the Balmoral servants downstairs for disco parties. But the real dancing challenge for Diana in her first Balmoral holiday was the Ghillies' Ball. For this annual party, Diana and the royal ladies pin tartan sashes over their dresses, lace up little leather slippers and join the kilted Princes to kick up their heels in noisy, whooping Highland style with the estate workers. The Queen Mother, the Queen and all the Windsors know the intricate steps and whooping etiquette. Diana may have to take lessons.

Christmas sees its own, very private royal ritual at Windsor Castle. Diana's first Noel as a Princess was a great contrast to the previous year, when she had caught 'flu and had to sniff through her family festivities at Althorp. She also had to stay away from her fiancé-to-be at Sandringham in the New Year, for the Norfolk estate was crawling with newshounds who had broken the sacred no-press rule in those hectic Diana-chasing days. On the arm of her husband in Christmas '81, she joined the ever-swelling flock of Windsors, Kents and Gloucesters who spilled down the steps of old St George's Chapel. The day followed the same royal blue print as Christmas past and set the pattern for Christmas to come. She and Charles install themselves in their castle apartment which shares a sitting-room with the rooms of all the Queen's children. Close by, in one of the Norman towers known as the 'Queen's tower', is the modern 'house' recently built for the Queen and the Duke. The family makes, or sometimes arranges, its own entertainment. In 1981 Charles invited 100 members of the Bach Choir to the castle and joined in their hymns and carols. But on December 24, the wrapping paper rattles *en masse* throughout the royal apartments; all gifts for adults are exchanged and the tree is lit on Christmas Eve, leaving Christmas morning free for church. Gifts are set out on a large table, partitioned by coloured ribbon for each person's pile. The Duke of Windsor once called the royal Christmas ''Dickens in a Cartier setting'', and though the family scene is no less Dickensian these days, very little from Cartier changes hands. The Queen insists she wants no more than ''a pound or two'' spent on her presents—one royal command which is broken with impunity. Among Diana's gifts from the Queen was probably a page-a-day diary, something the matriach gives her children every year to encourage maintenance of the age-old royal habit of diary-keeping. The Queen calls her lockable book her ''most secret friend''. Diana is said to dislike writing, even to herself. Charles, on the other hand, is the most methodical diarist

She shall have cameras wherever she goes

in the family, and often exceeds his daily page with typed additions.

The elders of the Royal Family treat Diana with a carefulness which is perhaps a fifty-fifty blend of affection and nervousness. They do not at all times approve of her whims, and for her part Diana is often stifled by the clan's eternal togetherness, particularly at Balmoral and Sandringham. According to one courtier, the Queen appears almost frightened of Diana at times. She is all too aware of Diana's power over the masses, yet the mother-in-law has never before had such close contact with a rock generation product whose personality and behaviour was not moulded by palaces and courts. To a large extent, Diana is an unknown quantity in the royal nest. They may find her undisciplined at times—leaping up in the middle of an endless dinner to plonk herself unceremoniously on her husband's lap while the servants tut-tut. But they also see her rightfully unimpressed by traditions in the lives of the Windsors and generations of royal ancestors that no one has ever challenged before. Diana's small defiances will be accepted, even enjoyed, in the Palace. But a wary eye will be kept on her. For now, she is handled as a piece of slightly funky Dresden, with tolerance and care. The Queen has had very little freedom in her own life and, as illustrated by her plea for a less intrusive press, she is anxious that Diana should not lose the last vestiges of her freedom a second before the consort's crown rests on her head.

By supporting him she gives him strength

TEN

Future Queen

"He is a man who will be made or marred by his wife"

COUNTESS OF STRATHMORE

"CHARLES has got himself a good Queen," my taxi-driver said without prompting at Buckingham Palace. To venture a "not yet, mate," would have seemed treasonable to this loyalist, who declared solemnly that Queen Elizabeth would "advocate" in a few years. Retirement at 60 is logical enough when three million are looking for jobs in Britain. But there is nothing logical about the continued existence of monarchy in a nation that gave the world trade unions, compulsory retirement and is today socialist in all but name. But logical practices cannot be expected within an establishment still using horsedrawn carriages, whose footmen still wear periwigs and livery, and whose very existence was once based on something as illogical as Divine Right. To pension off a monarch by the same rules as a government clerk is to say that a Queen is no different from the clerk; that Windsor blood is no bluer than any other. It may be true. But say it in a London pub and you could go home with a black eye. Britain may support freedom of speech, but the monarchy is one of the few institutions whose attackers are attacked. A man who displayed a painting of his conception of a nude Princess of Wales in his shop had his windows smashed by upright citizens—an insult to Diana is an insult to every Briton's wife, daughter or sister.

The monarchy has not always been so well loved. Its popularity has increased in direct relation to the decrease in power. Now that their kings and queens are politically impotent, Britons are able to love them to the point—as seen during the Queen's Jubilee and

119

Charles's and Diana's wedding—of hysteria. Monarchs now reign, if reign is the right word, as figureheads. Human nature requires an unflinching symbol of the nation's unity, its present and past and as an assurance that God is looking after the future. This security is not provided by abdicators. It is paradoxical, then, that no matter what the opinion polls say people want, the Queen's pledge to give them the service they need will prevent her abdication. She is healthy enough to make old bones. Barring accidents, the Prince and Princess of Wales will not wear the coronation robes until they are well into middle age. Diana will not be a radiant glamour girl by then, but some things about her will not have changed.

Just as Queen Elizabeth—who often takes dinner on a tray in front of television—contrasts with Queen Mary (she wore evening dress and tiara even when dining alone with her King), Queen Diana will reflect her times. After more than 30 years in the public eye, Queen Elizabeth's personality has remained a mystery to her subjects. But people will feel they know Queen Diana personally. In her first year of exposure, press delvings presented detailed (and sometimes accurate) run-downs on her domestic habits, her hobbies, her tastes in fashion, food, alcohol, and even her favourite expressions. There can be few people in the English-speaking world who did not learn of Diana's tendency to morning sickness and cravings for sweeties during pregnancy. Despite Prince Philip's suggested regular press conferences at the Palace, and both his and Charles's ease with occasional press audiences, the Queen has never faced the question—answer style interview. Neither has she ever appeared greatly at ease during her televised Christmas messages. Charles and Diana set the precedent for a media-star monarchy with television interviews and press sessions in the year following their engagement. Admittedly, the content was sugary stuff, vetted before and after by the Prince and watched, if we are to believe the story, by the Queen from behind a screen. But the step has been taken, one small step for Charles and Diana and a giant leap towards the real world for monarchy.

By the time she is Queen, then, people will feel, rightly or wrongly, that they know her so well she must be one of them. Thousands of her generation will be able to say they went to school with her. Hundreds will recall being at the hairdressers when the Princess of Wales was under the blow-drier. Dozens will know she took them to the loo at kindergarten and a whole generation will have worn the same brand of blue jeans she used to

The official photograph following the Queen's formal consent to the marriage

knock about in. No one can say that about any previous queen, and few can identify very strongly with Charles.

The Countess of Strathmore, Elizabeth Bowes Lyon's mother, looked at the stiff, inhibited Duke of York, and said: ''I do hope he will find a nice wife who will make him happy ... he is a man who will be made or marred by his wife.'' Bertie got his Elizabeth and an unwanted crown, and Lady Strathmore's prophecy was proven. The fun-loving Elizabeth softened his reserve, smoothed over his real and imagined inadequacies and made the reluctant Duke the most popular king of the century. It was the wife who shaped George VI and the monarchy into the calm and gentle influence that an unstable era cried out for. Diana will be the humanising element that will mould the monarchy for what the 21st century will demand of it.

But she will have to balance her act carefully. Britons may want to identify more closely with tomorrow's Royal Family, but they probably do not want to see them at roller-discos or riding bicycles in the Palace courtyard. The success of this most resilient royal line has surely lain in distancing itself from the masses in diminishing, but still discernible, degrees. This provides the element of mystique and glamour for those who want to believe Windsor blood is different from their own, that monarchs are far removed from their mundane lives. Hence the careful, sometimes worried, way the Queen may watch her daughter-in-law boogying downstairs in the servants' disco.

Charles travelled the world to find next door a wife with such star quality that now he and his mother must stand back to let crowds cheer for Diana. If other royal women are slighted, the Queen is not. It is exactly what she anticipated, even if the public love affair has gone on for longer than she expected. With true royal pragmatism—the trademark of any survivor—she steps aside as photographers dart past her towards Diana. ''I know what you want,'' she smiles. She knows, too, that if this daughter-in-law's whims are curbed, if the adulation is channelled, the Royal Family has in Diana its ticket into the next century, when it will be graciously waving from carriages as another Prince of Wales makes a royal tour of the Moon. Looking at Charles these days, it often seems as if he is walking in a dizzy, happy haze. He has not been by-passed by the effect Diana is having on the masses; the changes in the Prince of Wales are obvious to his friends and staff. They say he is more easy-going, less thrown by minor hitches.

He has varied the routine with his hairdressers of ten years' standing—the pukka Truefitt and Hill establishment in Old Bond Street—and sometimes has Diana's stylist round to the Palace to keep him in trim. He and his steeplechaser Good Prospect have finally parted company, to the relief of everyone from the Queen to the Palace spokesperson. Charles no longer has to prove he is one of the boys and not some namby-pamby Prince Fauntleroy, by nearly breaking his neck in every he-man sport going. He has a wife that half the men in the world covet, and he has fathered a child. He has been seen taking tap-dancing lessons from his wife. The Prince used to have a fettish about early rising, believing a moment in bed in the morning was a moment wasted. From the time of his honeymoon, he started seeing the light. And ignoring

122

Prince Charles used to recoil at the sight of babies

it. Emotionally, he is loosening up. The kiss on the hand that had the masses gasping below the balcony on his wedding day is such a frequent display these days that it barely merits pictures. Now when he dances with his wife on Highgrove's front lawn, even the ebullient Prince Andrew looks away in embarrassment. Once, when mothers attempted to foist their babies on to the Prince of Wales, he backed away, hands rigid in the stay where-you-are command. Now he zeros in on anything in a layette and calls his wife over to join the tiny talk. He says his wife is trying to fatten him up. She may succeed, for he abandoned the fanatic dieting of the steeplechasing days around the time he decided he could prove his manhood in less arduous ways than riding in the Grand National.

The Prince and Princess leave London for a Caribbean holiday

Diana has changed, too. Most obviously, pregnancy aside, there is a great deal less to the Princess of Wales than the Lady Diana who stepped, cheeks rounded with the last vestiges of puppy fat, on to the Palace lawn for the engagement pictures. ''You've got thin,'' hat-maker John Boyd opened Diana's coat and declared,

124

She keeps up with Charles at salmon fishing

with a candour that might have shortened his career, even his neck, in earlier royal times. "The word for it is slim," Diana replied, arch-primly. "My husband likes me this way." Charles's motto, apart from *Ich Dien*, is the E F Schumacher adage "small is beautiful". Apparently it applies to wives, too.

In the space of a year, Diana eased herself comfortably into high fashion. While that scandalous black opera dress and even that puff of ivory bridal silk seemed almost to take hold of Diana in their boned bodices and to wear her, she is now truly mistress of her own wardrobe and boss of her own style. Despite her inability to make a bad picture, she is more in charge of the press hordes who terrorised her early days in the limelight. They used to sit on her car, eat their lunches and call her Di. Now, in the unlikely event of their being presented to the Princess of Wales, Duchess of Cornwall, Countess of Chester and Baroness Renfrew, etc., they must bow and call her Ma'am. She took a perverse pleasure in pulling rank when she arrived in Port Said to face the cameras for the first time after her wedding. Every picture editor in Britain had briefed photographers and held the front page for a relaxed-lovers-on-the-deck snap. Charles accepted the symbiotic relationship between press and royalty, and did a creditable imitation of a casual stroll along *Britannia*'s deck. Diana—Shy Di, Sunny Di, Happy Di, Dinky Di and Daring Di—had had her share of newspaper clichés. She crammed her hat down over her eyes and

*Diana glances over her shoulder the day before her wedding. She
has never looked back since*

strode along the deck at valkyrie speed. All anybody photographed was a blur of brown legs and Bermuda shorts. Disappearing Di, shy like a hurricane. She has also played the odd little trick on photographers which raised the question of who will control the shutter on future royal coverage. Seeing a photographer who had haunted her pre-marital days, and noticing that he was temporarily without his camera at the polo, Diana leaped into the Prince of Wales's arms and nearly knocked him over with the smack of her kiss. Charles was still reeling when her giggles directed his gaze to the shell-shocked cameraman who had missed the shot of the month and would be too ashamed to tell anybody.

She who stoops to tricks also stoops to conquer. When a photographer dropped his lens over the crowd barrier and at her feet in Brixton, she bent down and handed it back so he could continue clicking profitably as she walked past. Naturally, the story of Princess Di's good deed made front pages. There are times when it seems she can win hearts simply by breathing.

Returning to the Young England Kindergarten as she sometimes did in the first year of her marriage, Diana saw the same toddlers who had crawled all over her and tugged at her cotton dress grow gradually more awed by this mythical creature they saw diamond-spangled on television. For better or worse, until death does them part, she is royal now in everyone's eyes.

There was talk, when people first puzzled over the unlikely ring of 'Queen Diana', that the name had a glossiness ill-becoming majesty. That in 25 years or so, when she became Queen, some Palace stuffed-shirt would come up with something more regal. But though she will never be known as anything but Princess of Wales until she becomes Queen, she still signs her name Diana. When the crowds call for her, the name they scream is Diana. And if her public following continues with the same passion as in her first year as Princess of Wales, the name Diana will have taken on a regal aura of its own by the time Charles is crowned. Let anybody try to call the next consort anything but Queen Diana.

Acknowledgements

The author acknowledges the assistance of the office of the Prince and Princess of Wales and the Buckingham Palace press office in the writing of this book; in particular, the help and advice of Michael Shea and Warwick Hutchings.

Special thanks are also due to the Garter King of the College of Arms, London, and his staff; Patrick Montague-Smith, former editor of Debrett; John Boyd, milliner of note; hairdresser Kevin Shanley; designers David Sassoon and Belinda Bellville and the staff of the Crown Agents. The author also thanks Anwar Hussein, photographer, for invaluable research, aid and encouragement. Thanks, too, to a discreet cluster of contacts who would not appreciate being thanked by name.

Most of the pictures in this book were taken by Anwar Hussein. Other pictures have been used as follows:
Associated Newspapers 6, 47, 125, Ron Burton 59, Central Press 9, 31, Country Life 38, Crown Copyright 63, Kent Gavin 55, Tim Graham 5, 95, 111, David Graves 107, Robin Gray 67, Keystone 37, 89, **109 (bottom)**, Lichfield 2, Mike Lloyd **81**, 118, Mike Maloney 124, National Portrait Gallery 83, Desmond O'Neill 35, Photo Library 88, 103, Press Association 4, 12, 15, 23, 41, 42, 43, 58, 69, 87, 93, 96, 114, 121, 126, Syndication International 48.

The following Commonwealth Countries have issued stamps bearing the likeness of the Princess of Wales:
Ascension Island, Bahamas, Barbados, British Antarctic Territory, British Virgin Islands, Cayman Islands, Falkland Islands, Falkland Island Dependencies, Fiji, The Gambia, Lesotho, Mauritius, Pitcairn Islands, St Helena, Solomon Islands, Swaziland, Tristan da Cunha.